King David Lives Again!

(WHY Americans, and the Wise People of the Whole World, Want a Righteous KING to Govern them!)

By

The Worldwide People's Revolution!®

Book 142 ♦

(The Cover Photo shows an Innocent Baby.
Could it be the Reincarnation of King David?)

Jer 30:9   But they shall serve the LORD their God, and David
their king, whom I will raise up unto them.

Copyright, Dedication and Introduction

By our Selected King's Chief Editor —
Dr. Samuel Walker Edison, Ph.D., M.A., BS and QC!

ISBN — 13: 979-8573-5732-12

00-01 [_] This Inspired Book is COPYRIGHTED 2020, by **The Worldwide People's Revolution!** All Rights are Reserved for the Truth's Sake. However, you, or anyone else, has the Right to Reproduce Exact Copies of this Wonderful little Book, and Sell them to whomever might Want them, and KEEP 90% of the Net Profits: beCause, our Selected King only wants 10% of the Net Profits for the Construction of "The Great World TEMPLE of PEACE!" (The Glory of Jerusalem Arises Again in the Great State of Flexible Texas!) By The Worldwide People's Revolution!® Book 017B, which will be the HEADQUARTERS for "The New RIGHTEOUS One-World Government!" (HOW to Establish a Righteous One-World Government without Going to WAR!) By The Worldwide People's Revolution!® Book 056, which will be the Tallest and Largest Building in the entire World: beCause, it will House all of the Elected Officials from all Nations, who will Liv within "Beautiful Swanky Stone Dome Home COMPLEXES!" (HOW to Build SECURE Tax-proof, Insurance-proof, Self-air-conditioned, Paint-proof, Rot-proof, Termite-proof, Mouse-proof, Fireproof, Tornado-proof, Hurricane-proof, Thief-proof, and BOMB-PROOF Houses!) By The Worldwide People's Revolution!® Book 102, which will Set a Good Example for the Wise People of all Nations, who will keep themselves Busy by Building those "GLORIOUS Swanky Hotels Castles and Fortresses!" (Beautiful Planned City States for WISE Intelligent Well-Educated People with Common Sense and Good Understanding!) By The Worldwide People's Revolution!® Book 019B, with the Assistance of "Seven Great Armies of Working Soldiers!" (HOW to Provide a Way for Everyone to WORK: so as to Eliminate Poverty, Crimes, Drug Abuses, Prisons and Unnecessary Taxes!) By The Worldwide People's Revolution!® Book 015B: beCause, the Tax Slaves are Sick of "Poverty Hunger Riots Strikes Police Brutalities Election Deceptions and Civil Wars!" (The High Price that we Earthlings have Paid for Leaving the Good Land!) By The Worldwide People's Revolution!® Book 014B. After all, this is "The END of CONFUSION!" (The Great CELEBRATION of the Magnificent Wedding of the Most-Humble, Honest Nations, and the Grand Year of JUBILEE!) By The Worldwide People's Revolution!® Book 050, which is more Thoroughly Explained in "HOW Righteousness can Overcome Wickedness!" (The Triumph of the Soul who Knows God!) By The Enlightened Professor of Common Sense! Book 093, who is the Inspired Author of more than 364 Exceptionally Good Books, which Explain "The Worldwide People's Revolution!" (A Comprehensive Plan for Obtaining Worldwide Law, Order, Obedience, Peace and True Prosperity!) By The Worldwide People's Revolution!® Book 108, since "All of the Arguments are in Favor of our Selected King, who has Zero Challengers!" (Before you Attend another Election Deception, you should Carefully Study this Inspired Book with an Honest Open Mind!) By The Worldwide People's Revolution!® Book 085, which is a Companion Book of: "101 Good Reasons and Great Advantages for Establishing a Righteous One-World Government!" (Government By the People, Of the People, and For the People!) By The Worldwide People's Revolution!® Book 104. Yes, "Our Selected King SPEAKS OUT!" (It is High Time for some Sane Person to get

Total Control of this Insane World!) By The Worldwide People's Revolution!® Book 100. Therefore, be Wise, O Electors, and "VOTE for The GOAT!" (The New Political Party that has Guaranteed Solutions for our Massive Problems!) By The Worldwide People's Revolution!® Book 109, even if it Sounds too Good to be True: beCause, our Selected King Offers a ONE-MILLION-DOLLAR REWARD to anyone who can Prove his "Guaranteed Solutions!" (HOW to Solve our Local and Global Problems in the Most-Rational Manner Possible!) By The Worldwide People's Revolution!® Book 080, to be WRong or Unworkable!‡

00-02 [_] The Normal American Wooden / Plastic Firetrap Mouse-infested Cockroach Den costs 150 to 250 thousand Dollars, and has the Value of the one that is Pictured above, which will Cost even more Time, Money, and Energy, just to Clean Up the Big Capitalist MESS, which was 10,000 Times Worse in Paradise, California, in 2018, after a Wildfire Reduced it to Ashes and Trash: beCause, their Extremely Ignorant Federal Government did not Explain the Facts of Life to those Poor Children, whereby they might have Built Good Fireproof Houses for themselves, and not Suffered any Losses of Lives nor Properties. However, according to Senator Blabbermouth III, that would be Bad for the Insurance Business, the Lumber Companies, and the Producers of Trash. Indeed, the 80 or so People who Died in the Wildfire were of no Great Concern to the Big-mouthed Trumpeter, who Blamed it onto the Governor of Californicate, who Failed to "clean up the woods." None of them ever took the Time to Study: "HOW to DEFEAT Wild Fires, Systematically!" (A Scientific Method for Conquering the Enemy!) By The Worldwide People's Revolution!® Book 133: beCause, "Cave houses are not very popular," they say, as if a Beautiful Billion-dollar Swanky Stone Dome Home Complex were a Dark Damp Dank Damned CAVE House in the Overgrown Jungle of Self-Inflicted Torments! Nothing could be Farther from the TRUTH of it! ‡

00-03 [_] For Example, there is a Small Portion of the Shrine of Immaculate Conceptions in Washington, District of Chief Criminals, which is not in Danger of any Wildfires: beCause, Concrete, Rocks, Ceramic Tiles, Polished Marble Tiles, and Granite Columns are not Threatened by Fires; but, that Good News never got into the *Holy Bible,* which is supposed to be "The Primary Instruction Manual for Mankind to Live by," according to the Irreverent LOUDMOUTH Slothgut Windbag Hole-in-Thy-Head. But, the Doubters might say that *the Declaration of Independence* and our Constitution for "The Divided States of United Lies!" (The so-called "United States of North America" in Disguise!) By The Worldwide People's Revolution!® Book 058, are the Embodiment of All that is GOOD, which is GOD; but, where in the Declaration or Constitution does it Mention anything about True Prosperity? Our Selected King has a much Better Constitution, and a *Declaration of Interdependence,* which far Outshines all others, even as this Inspired Book Far Outshines anything that comes Out of "The BIG White OUTHOUSE on the Not-so-Biblical Capitol DUNGHILL!" (The Chief Sins of the Divided States of United Lies!) By The Worldwide People's Revolution!® Book 023B, which Reeks with Ancient Elephant Droppings and Fresh Political Donkey Dung, from the Dank Basement to the Head of the Statue of Fake Freedom at the Top of the Cast Iron Dome, who LOUDLY Proclaims Liberty throughout all of the Land, unto the Education Slaves, Work Slaves, Tax Slaves, Rent Slaves, Home-owner Slaves, Interest Slaves, Insurance Slaves, Mortgage Slaves, ElecTrickery Bills Slaves, Food Bills Slaves, Water Bills Slaves, Gas Bills Slaves, Transportation Bills Slaves, Repair Bills Slaves, Telephone Bills Slaves, Internet Bills Slaves, Entertainment Bills Slaves, Drug Bills Slaves, Doctor Bills Slaves, Hospital Bills Slaves, Childcare Bills Slaves, Nursing Home Bills Slaves, and Funeral Home Bills Slaves: beCause, the Great FALSE Economy is nothing more than a Well-Camouflaged SLAVERY SYSTEM for Ignorant Fools to Believe in, who will no doubt Speak Evil of our Selected King, and call him a "Communist," "Socialist," "Tyrant," "the Anti-Christ,"

or "Satan, h i m s e l f"! Yes, they are as Superstitious as those Deceived Muslims, who Vainly Imagine that MuhamMAD Rode a White Horse with 4 little Wings on a Prayer Rug to Heaven! But, you and I just Happen to Know Better, Right? Well, you may Judge this Subject for yourself, after you have Learned all of the Evidences: beCause, our Selected King Speaks the Provable TRUTHS that can Liberate all of us from the Prison of Capitalist Lies, and Bless all of us Believers with those "Beautiful Swanky Stone Dome Home COMPLEXES!" (HOW to Build SECURE Tax-proof, Insurance-proof, Self-air-conditioned, Paint-proof, Rot-proof, Termite-proof, Mouse-proof, Fireproof, Tornado-proof, Hurricane-proof, Thief-proof, and BOMB-PROOF Houses!) By The Worldwide People's Revolution!® Book 102. Yes, you must Strain yourself to Believe it, O Unbeliever: beCause, it is True that God Provided a Way for us to do that! †§‡§§

00-04 [_] Yes, God Generously Provided hundreds of thousands of Mountains of Rocks for us to Play with, if we are Wise, along with Metals, Minerals, Sand, Gravel, Water, Oils, Gases, Tools and Technologies to Work with; but, the Honest Slave says, "I could never afford to buy a billion-dollar house. I barely earn enough money to pay my present bills." Exactly! You are just another Mistreated SLAVE, who is Trapped in an EVIL Capitalist FALSE Economic System; but, would Liars Confess it? Would they Humble themselves to Confess that our Selected King is RIIT? NO, never! — beCause, they are Obviously BRAINWASHED with Capitalist LIES! Therefore, they should Stop Trying to Justify the Great False Economy: beCause, it will only Blind their Minds. ‡

00-05 [_] O Doctor Samuel Walker Edison, I must Humble myself and Confess that you and your Selected King are Correct; but, we Americans do NOT BELIEVE IN KINGS, which is WHY that we just recently Elected another Powerless President, who must get the Permission of the CONgress and of the Low Court of Supreme Injustices, just to get anything Done in Government! But, since our Constitution does not Mention what True Prosperity is, I am Wondering if we are making any True Progress, at all? {See: "What is True PROGRESS???" (Are we Making any

 Does the *Holy Bible* Explain what True Progress is, O Doctor Sam? Where would a Person Learn the Whole Truth about it all, if not from the *Holy Bible?* Can we Trust our Reason and Logic to get it Riit? ‡

00-06 [_] Well, my Friend, the Capitalists would like everyone to Believe that they should Own a Big Mansion on the Hilltop with 4 or more Garages with Expensive Automobiles in them, and perhaps a Helicopter for Riding to the Airport to get into their Jet Airplane, and go on a Cruise over the Bahamas; but, you can easily Understand that it is a Dead-end Street for 99.999,999,999% of the People, who do well to Own a Used Trailer House with some Dumpy Old Rusty Car with an almost Empty Gas Tank, Bald Tires, and Worn-out Seats, some of whom have 6,000$-worth of Credit Card Debts, the Third Mortgage on the Wooden / Plastic Firetrap House, and a Child or 2 with Down's Syndrome, Epilepsy, Polio, Cancer, or something Worse: beCause of not Eating Wholesome Natural Foods and Drinks, as Jesus Christ and the Apostle Paul would have them do.

00-07 [_] O Doctor Sam, I would Like to do my Shopping at the Whole Foods Market; but, the Prices are about one-third Higher than some Dumpy Grocery Store on the South Side of Town. Therefore, being a Prisoner of Society, and in Debt Up to my little Tally Whacker, what am I supposed to Do to Fix it? Does your Selected King have "Guaranteed Solutions!" (HOW to Solve our Local and Global Problems in the Most-Rational Manner Possible!) By The Worldwide People's Revolution!® Book 080? If so, I will "VOTE for The GOAT!" (The New Political Party that has Guaranteed Solutions for our Massive Problems!) By The Worldwide

People's Revolution!® Book 109, in the Year 2024. However, in the Meantime, those All-American Wooden / Plastic Firetrap Mouse-infested Cockroach Dens will be going Up to Heaven in Great Billowing Black Clouds of TOXIC SMOKE, and Radical Climate Changes will Produce more Deadly and Destructive Tornadoes, Hurricanes, Wildfires, Erupting Volcanoes, Earthquakes, and whatever Satan Blesses us with. However, if we were Wise, we would Elect a Righteous KING, who would Invite his **"Seven Great Armies of Working Soldiers!" (HOW to Provide a Way for Everyone to WORK: so as to Eliminate Poverty, Crimes, Drug Abuses, Prisons and Unnecessary Taxes!) By The Worldwide People's Revolution!® Book 015B**, to Build those **"GLORIOUS Swanky Hotels Castles and Fortresses!" (Beautiful Planned City States for WISE Intelligent Well-Educated People with Common Sense and Good Understanding!) By The Worldwide People's Revolution!® Book 019B**: beCause, they just Happen to have more than 5,000 Good Reasons and Great Advantages for Building them: beCause, they are "The Right Design for Living!" (A List of Great Advantages for Building Beautiful Planned City States!) By The Worldwide People's Revolution!® Book 012B. However, the Spiritually Deaf People cannot Hear it, nor do they Want to Understand it: beCause, they only Want to Carry on as Normal, and have a Party at the Expense of their Great Grandchildren, who will be Burdened with all of our National Debts, if they Survive **"The Great ATOMIC NIGHTMARE!" (The Saddest Story in World History!) By The Great White Bald Eagle! Book 099**. Therefore, what is to be Done for them? Who can Save them from their Capitalist MADNESS? *"Pride comes Parading itself in Front of Destruction, and a Haughty Spirit in Front of a Fall,"* as King Solomon Warned! †§‡§§

00-08 [_] Well, my Friend, only a Righteous KING can Save us from Destruction, and only if he has the Cooperation of the Masses of People, who must Learn what all that he Proposes, before they Juj it, or Condemn him for Proposing it, while Fearing the Establishment of a RIGHTEOUS One-World Government, in spite of the Fact that there are more than **"101 Good Reasons and Great Advantages for Establishing a Righteous One-World Government!" (Government By the People, Of the People, and For the People!) By The Worldwide People's Revolution!®** Book 104. After all, he is not Asking us to Say nor Do any Evil Things; but, if you Think so, please Send your Complaint to the E-Mail Address that you can Find on the Outside of the Back Cover, near to the Bottom of the Page. Just Watch this YouTube Video, and then tell me that we have no Need for such a Good Government: **https://youtu.be/2Ci0q-r7RHw Tsunamis — Danger from the Depths of Hell!** Yes, you can go from there to a thousand similar YouTube Videos about Natural Disasters, Capitalist Trash, Air Pollution, Water Pollution, etc. *"Seek, and you will Find."*

00-09 [_] O Doctor Sam, all of those YouTube Videos Upset the Belly of my Mind: beCause, I have no **"Guaranteed Solutions,"** as you and your Selected King have. Moreover, I cannot Visualize any **"GLORIOUS Swanky Hotels Castles and Fortresses!" (Beautiful Planned City States for WISE Intelligent Well-Educated People with Common Sense and Good Understanding!) By The Worldwide People's Revolution!®** Book 019B, in my Weak Mind. §‡

00-10 [_] Well, my Friend, our Selected King will Help you to Visualize it, if you simply Study this Inspired Book, by Reading it 3 or 4 Times with an Open Mind, which you can Do by Persuading your Friends and Naaberz to Reed it to you, in spite of any "Mispeld Werdz," which are written Phonetically, liik thaa Sownd. {See: **"Justifications for Writing Styles!" (Why our Selected King Writes so Strangely!) By The Worldwide People's Revolution!®** Book 129.} §

The Appetizing MENU on the Table of Contents for a Satisfying Feast of Entertaining Truths!

This Inspired Book contains about 25,000 Words of Provable Truths for Wise People with Open Minds, plus a few Colored Photographs with Explanations for your Education and Enlightenment.

Explanations for Symbols:

† The Dagger represents *the Sword of Controversies,* which Means that someone Disagrees with the Statement. You may put your own large Dagger wherever you Want, if you Disagree with it.

‡ The Double Dagger represents *the Double-edged Sword of Controversies,* which Means that the Statement must be Proven at: "The GREAT Worldwide TELEVISED Court HEARING!" (That Great Meeting of the Most-Intelligent and Well-Educated Minds!) By The Worldwide People's Revolution!® Book 041B, which is otherwise known as, **"The GWTCH!"** or Witch! §

§ The Section Symbol represents *Sarcastic Statements.* Two such Symbols (§§) Together, means that the Statement is so Sarcastic that it Proves itself to be WRong. For Example, the Fake Trumpeter Lost the Election Deception; but, he did not Lose his Faithful Followers, who would Happily Die for him, just to Keep him in Power as a Powerless President, who does not even have a Remedy for the Bug-19, which is Revealed in the *Holy Bible,* which most Preachers have not Discovered: beCause they Fail to Believe it and Practice what it Teaches: beCause they are Followers of the Fake Trumpeter, who has never Red it with a Capital R, nor even a small r. ‡§‡§§

— Chapter 01 —

Righteous Anointed Kings
versus
Powerless Elected Presidents!

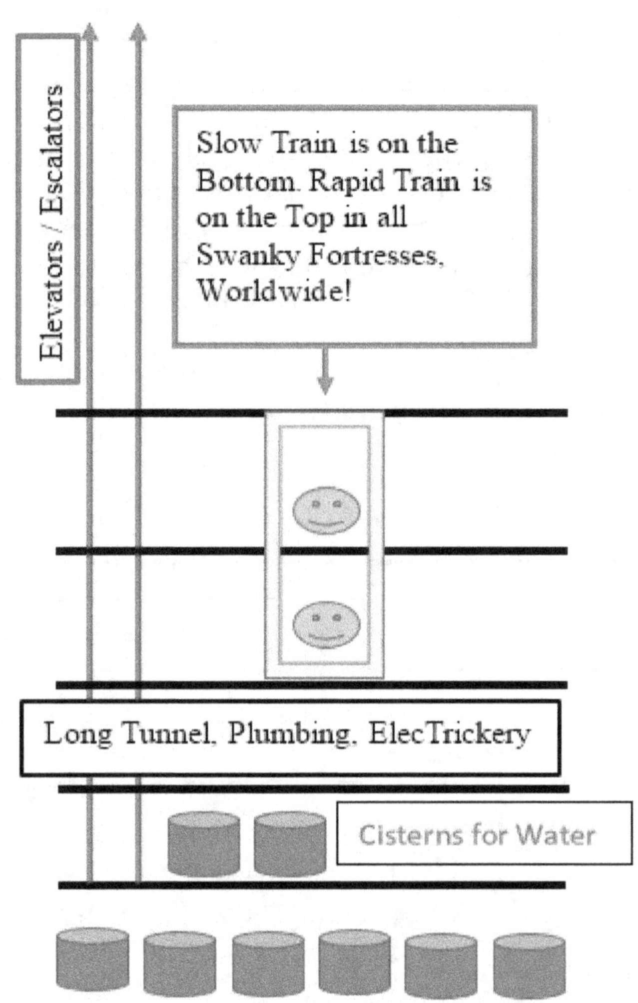

01-01 [_] Most People do not Know it, even as I did not Know it for more than 30 Years; but, those "**GLORIOUS Swanky Hotels Castles and Fortresses!**" just Happen to have more than 5,000 Advantages over normal Cities of Confusion! For Example, they use Elevators, Escalators, and Electric Subway Trains, instead of Expensive, DANGEROUS, Polluting, Noisy, STINKING Greasy Cars, Pickup Trucks, Vans, Buses, Semi Trucks, and other ABOMINATIONS, as God would Naturally call them: beCause, he has not Lost his Riit Mind, nor his Common Sense. For Example, all of the Roofs are Covered with Beautiful All-Mineral Organic Vegetable Gardens, Vineyards, Berry Bushes, Fruit Trees, Nut Trees, and Flower Gardens for Honey Bees and Pretty Butterflies to Feast on. Anyone who Objects to that Plan has simply not Thot it over very Well. ‡

01-02 [_] O Selected King of "The New RIGHTEOUS One-World Government!" (HOW to Establish a Righteous One-World Government without Going to WAR!) By The Worldwide People's Revolution!® Book 056, would you have us Tax Slaves ABANDON and FORSAKE our Beautiful Crime-infested Cities of Confusion with their Wooden / Plastic Firetrap Mouse-infested Cockroach Dens, just to Liv in those "Beautiful Swanky Stone Dome Home COMPLEXES!" (HOW to Build SECURE Tax-proof, Insurance-proof, Self-air-conditioned, Paint-proof, Rot-proof, Termite-proof, Mouse-proof, Fireproof, Tornado-proof, Hurricane-proof, Thief-proof, and BOMB-PROOF Houses!) By The Worldwide People's Revolution!® Book 102, which no one could Afford to BUY? Have you Lost your Riit Mind, or what? I am a True Christian, just in case you do not Know it; and I say that it would be a Great SIN to Liv in Peace with other True Christians, and not have any Sinners around us, for us to Work on their Consciences, and get them Converted to the Teachings of Jesus Christ. For Example, how would we ever get Sinners, like Donald Jaywalking Trump, Converted to the Truth, if we did not Liv next-door to them, whereby we might Talk with them, in Private, while they are Hoeing the Weeds in their Backyard Chemical Gardens? Otherwise, we could Talk with their Consciences by Shouting Out the Gospel Truth from our Housetops; but, not in your False Economic System, which does not even Require Gas-hog Cars to Drive to Work in. You are Crazy! Therefore, I Suggest that you Study MY Plan, which is much more Practical, using Cars. †§‡§§

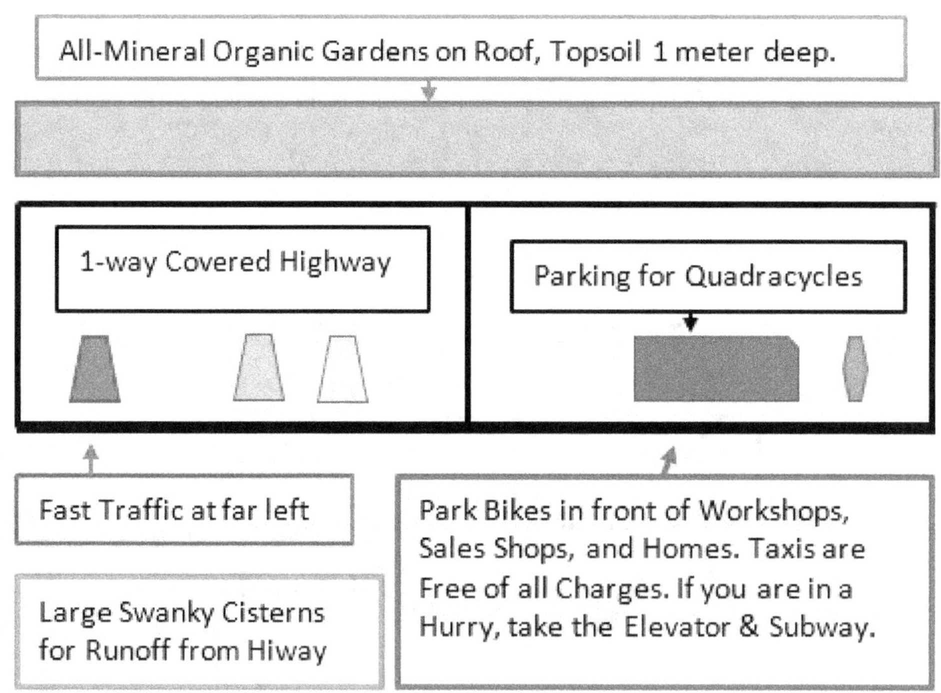

01-03 [_] Well, my Weak-minded Friend, with your Plan, there would still be those Hateful Accidents with Vehicles, as well as other Problems — such as a Lack of SECURITY, if the City were Bombed by an Enemy; but, with my Plan, there would be NO Ugly Highways, nor any Exposed Houses, Workshops, nor Sales Shops: beCause all of the Houses, Workshops and Sales Shops would be SECURE behind Tall THICK Stone Walls, which might be 60 to 200 feet Tall and 30 to 100 feet Thick at their Bases, just to make Bombing an Impractical Evil Deed: beCause, all of the Stone Dome Home Complexes would be Covered with 10 to 40 feet of Sand, Rough

1 Granite Rocks, Gravel, Rubble Rocks, Clay, and All-Mineral Organic Gardens with at least 3 feet
2 of Rich Topsoil for those Fruit Trees, Nut Trees, Grape Vines, Berry Bushes, Vegetable Gardens
3 and Flower Gardens, which would be Behind Secure Tall Stone Walls, whereby they would be
4 Protected from High Winds, Hail Storms, Killing Frosts, Acid Rains, and whatever Satan might
5 Send against us, according to *the Book of Jobe,* which Credits him with all such Evil Things. †§‡
6

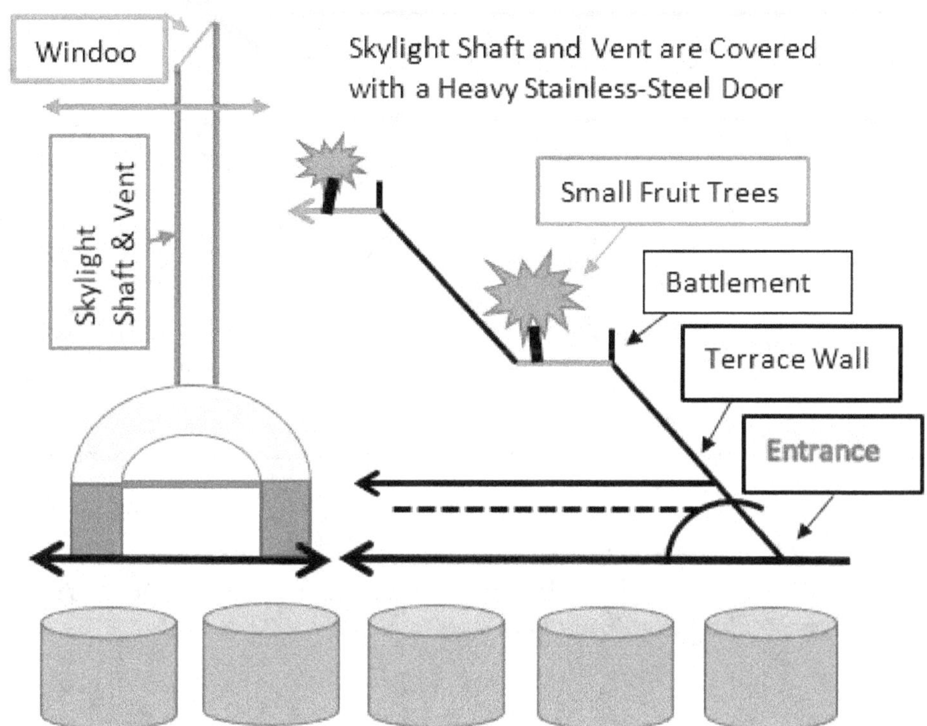

7
8
9 01-04 [_] O Selected King, just how many of those Short Stone Terraces would there be around a
10 Swanky Fortress? And where are the Greenhouse Glass and Steel Roofs that Cover the Fruit Trees?
11
12 01-05 [_] Well, my Friend, those are Drawings for Mild Semi-Tropical Climates, which do not
13 Need any Greenhouse Roofs; but, the Fruit Trees in the Terraces are Protected from High Winds,
14 which are Deflected by the Battlement Walls, if they are Tall enough. Indeed, the Tall Terrace
15 Walls will CATCH the Wind, and Funnel it toward the Top, while the Battlement Walls will
16 DEFLECT the Wind Over the Fruit Trees, Nut Trees, Grape Vines, Berry Bushes, or whatever is
17 Planted in those Short Terraces, which would only be Found *within* the Swanky Fortress, and NOT
18 on the Outside of it: beCause, the Outside must be Protected from Invaders, for which I have
19 another Plan. However, there are many Ways to Do such Things, and any of them will Work much
20 Better than the Present Plan, which has NO Protective Stone Walls, at all, as in the Case of
21 Paradise, California, which BURNED UP! Yes, it Killed some 80 Victims of Capitalism, and
22 Destroyed more than 10,000 Houses during just one Day! And that was just "a Preview of the
23 Horrible Movie to Come," you might say, which will Totally Wreck our Great False Economy. †‡
24
25 01-06 [_] O Selected King, I suggest that we Architects get Together with the Engineers, and make
26 our Best Plans, as if we had an Unlimited Supply of Good Money to Work with, as if we are

1 making a Beautiful Planned City State for Jesus Christ and his Disciples to Liv in, which must be
2 very SECURE and Safe for all of his Holy Children. Here, for Example, is HOW that I would
3 Build the Outer Wall around the Swanky Fortress, on the Outside of the Outer Moat, about 20
4 Miles from the GLORIOUS Swanky Fortress Wall, itself, which would Deter Army Tanks:
5

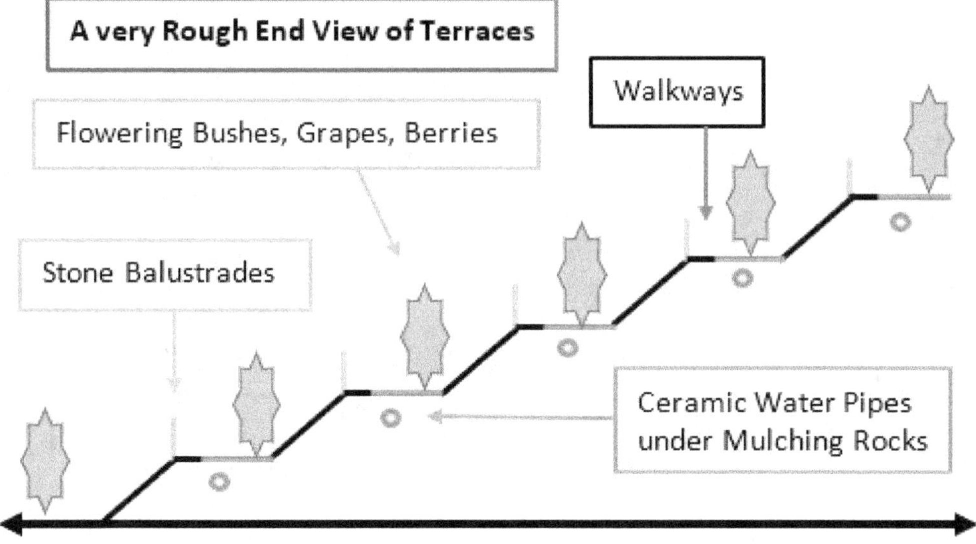

6
7
8 01-07 [_] So, my Friend, are you Suggesting that the entire Swanky Fortress should be Surrounded
9 by Fruit Trees, Nut Trees, Grape Vines, Berry Bushes, and Flowering Bushes? How would you
10 keep the Thieves from Stealing the Fruits and Nuts?
11

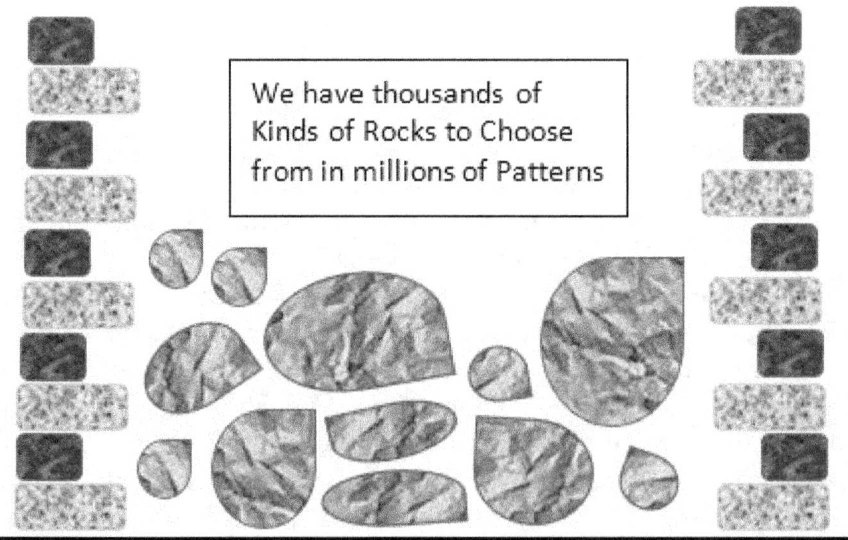

12
13
14 01-08 [_] Well, O Righteous King, I would not even Attempt to Deter any Thieves from Stealing
15 those Fruits nor Nuts; but, I would put up a Short Stone Wall with little Bedroom Domes and
16 Bathrooms right next to the Terraces, just on the Outside of the Fortress, which would have

1   Unlocked Doorways into those little Domes, with Signs on every Door, reading: **These small**
2   **Domes are Designed for Poor Hungry People to Stay in them, and Eat from the Fruit Trees**
3   **and Berry Bushes, until they have taken the Time to Reed the Books that are Provided for**
4   **Free by The Swanky Association of Compassionate Missionaries, who are having Mercy on**
5   **all such Poor People. Therefore, Stay as long as you Like, and Eat as much as you Want, and**
6   **Study those Special Books: beCause, it is Possible for you to Liv within a GLORIOUS**
7   **Swanky Fortress, and have no more Hateful Bills to Pay. Please Study the Pictures on the**
8   **Walls for Examples of how we Liv. Moreover, if you cannot Reed, please Ask someone to**
9   **Help you with the Reeding: beCause, they have nothing Better to Do with their Time.**
10

11
12
13   01-09 [_] So, my Friend, are you saying that you would Transform those Poor Beggars into
14   Helpless Welfare Victims, who would come from all Ends of the Earth, just to Eat on those Fruit
15   Trees and Nut Trees? Would they not be making a HUGE Trash Dump of the entire Territory?
16   Indeed, they would just Naturally be Packing in their Shopping Carts full of Plastic Bags for Potato
17   Chips, Coke Cans, Hair Sprays, Fly Sprays, and whatever else, just to Litter the whole Place:
18   beCause, they Obviously have no Respect for anything. Therefore, the Whole Territory would
19   soon Look like an African Trash Dump: beCause of having Freedom to Do whatever they Want
20   to, and without any Policemen to Watch over them. In Fact, Women and Girls would be getting
21   Raped, and Boys Sodomized by Wicked Old Men: beCause, WHO c/sh/would Restrain them? †§‡
22
23   01-10 [_] O Selected King, we could put up an UGLY Nazi Concentration Camp FENCE around
24   the Outside Wall with a Guard House every 200 Meters, or so, which would Restrict those Beggars
25   from Trashing the Place. In Fact, they could be Restrained from Packing anything into those little

1 Dome Homes, which could even have Beds and Recliners in them, as well as TV Screens for them
2 to Watch, whereby we might even Educate them a bit — that is, unless they are really Stupid
3 People, like the Fake Trumpeter and his Hardhearted Followers, who still Vainly Imagine that he
4 Won the Election Deception, in spite of Losing the Popular Vote by no less than 1.4 Billion Votes,
5 Worldwide! In Fact, the 160 Million Americans, who did not even bother to Vote, were Voting
6 against him and Dr. Josephine Beardless Biden, who has no "Guaranteed Solutions!" (HOW to
7 Solve our Local and Global Problems in the Most-Rational Manner Possible!) By The
8 Worldwide People's Revolution!® Book 080, for anything! But, we now have such Solutions. ‡
9

10
11
12 01-11 [_] Well, my Friend, I Think that you would do Well to just Shut Up and let me Explain
13 what is Best for all of us: beCause, I have Thot about all of these Things for more than 60 Years,
14 whereby I have had lots of Time to Figure it all Out, and come to the Best Conclusions. However,
15 I do Agree with you — that it would be a Good Idea to put an "Enticement" all around each
16 Swanky Fortress, just for the Shy People, who might be Afraid of Swanky Fortresses, who might
17 also bee Afraad tq Reed Goud Bouks, and especially if they are written in Funetik Ingglish, which
18 has one Way to Spell just one Sound, as opposed to 5, 10, or 20 Different Waaz to spel wun sownd.
19 For Example, the Vowel Sound of "OO" in School, is speld with a single U in Rule, a single O in
20 do, an OE in Shoe, OUGH in through, IOUX in Sioux Indian, EW in Crew, IEU in lieu, OU in
21 Group, HOU in Ghoul, OOH in pooh, HU in Rhubarb, HEU in Rheumatism, OUS in Rendezvous,

1 CIUT in Prosciutto, WO in two, UE in blue, and the List goes on and ON: beCause the Inventors
2 of English Spelling were Near Relatives of the Barbarians, who Failed to Understand that each
3 SOWND Needs a Consistent SYMBOL to Represent it, and only ONE such Simboul: beCause,
4 there is no Rational Reason for having 10 to 200 Different Ways to Spell a single Sound. †§‡§§
5

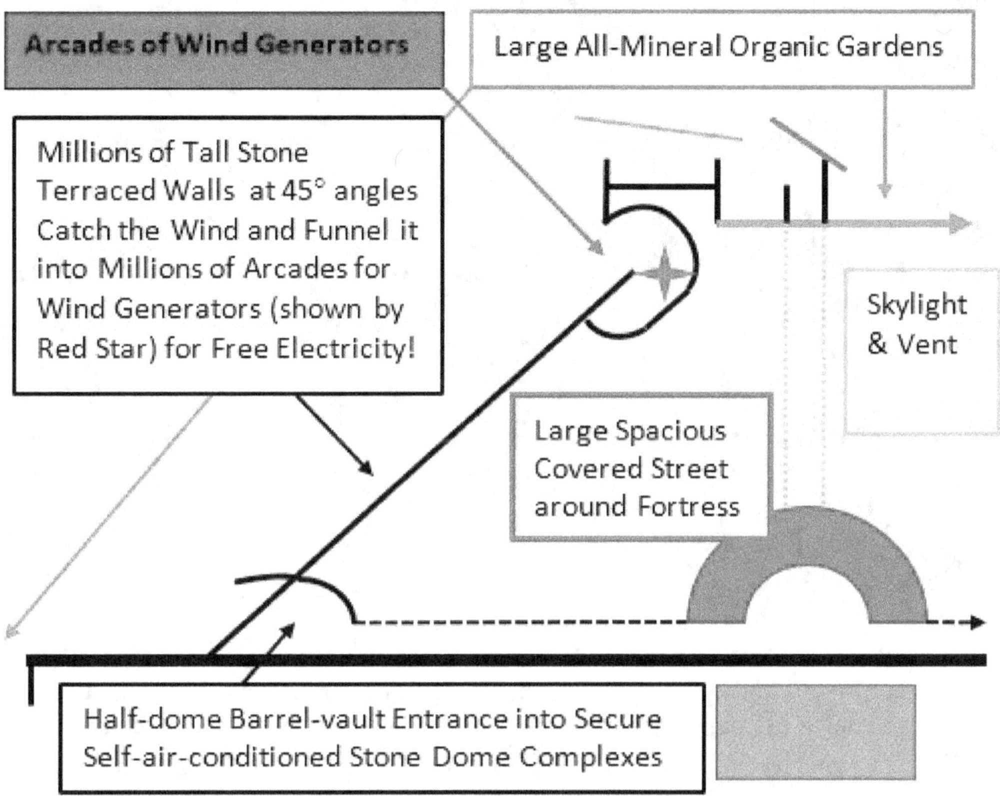

6
7
8 01-12 [_] So, O Selected King of "The New RIGHTEOUS One-World Government!" are you
9 Suggesting that we are all just Ignorant IDIOTS, who Desperately Need a Righteous KING to
10 Govern us, just to Deliver us from the MADNESS of Vain and Foolish Traditions? Is that King
11 DAVID Hiding somewhere behind the Berry Bushes? Or, must we Electors Discover someone
12 whom we can Call "King David," like the British do, and like the Catholic Church does for their
13 Popes? For Example, Pope Francis is not really Francis of Assisi; but, he is Jorge Mario Bergoglio
14 the Great, who is obviously Pregnant, even if he does not know it, who should Study: "The Proper
15 RULES for FASTING!" (The Complete Instruction Manual for True Repentance!) By The
16 Worldwide People's Revolution!® Book 046, which is a Companion Book of: "HOW to
17 Become a HOLY Man!" (40 Good Reasons WHY People Should FAST and PRAY!) By The
18 Worldwide People's Revolution!® Book 045, which is a Part of "An Amazing Collection of
19 Wit and Wisdom!" (The Marvelous Tale of the Colorful Peacock from Angel Ridge, and the
20 Strong Rope of Everlasting Hope!) By The Worldwide People's Revolution!® Book 048. Yes,
21 I just Finished Reading "The Peabrain Peacock Studies Demon-ocracy!" (A Guaranteed
22 Solution for the Plastic Trash Problem!) By The Worldwide People's Revolution!® Book
23 141, and I Think that if such an Inspired Book were Placed in those little Stone Domes for the
24 Beggars and Poor People, who are too Shy to Knock on the Door of a Swanky Fortress, they would
25 Reed it, and do their Best to keep the Place Clean and Livable, without anyone to Police them. †§‡

01-13 [_] Well, my Friend, you have a lot of Faith in Mankind; but, I do not: beCause, I have done quite a bit of Traveling, and have seen the Slums that Poor People have Managed, and they are not very Pretty Sites to Visit. However, if those same People were DRAFTED into **"Seven Great Armies of Working Soldiers!" (HOW to Provide a Way for Everyone to WORK: so as to Eliminate Poverty, Crimes, Drug Abuses, Prisons and Unnecessary Taxes!) By The Worldwide People's Revolution!®** Book 015B, when they are about 12 Years Old, they could easily be Trained to Liv like Civilized Human Beings; but, I am Sure that X-number of them would be Unhappy with that Plan for a Week or 2, until they got Accustomed to it; and then, like every Intelligent Person who ever Lived, they would Naturally LOVE IT! After all, how is one NOT going to Love the True Riches? Trust me, the Polished Marble Walls never get Boring, and never Need Painting, which, alone will easily Pay for them: beCause Paint is very Expensive, nowadays.

01-14 [_] O Selected King of "The Worldwide People's Revolution!" (A Comprehensive Plan for Obtaining Worldwide Law, Order, Obedience, Peace and True Prosperity!) By The Worldwide People's Revolution!® Book 108, I would Prefer to Liv in my Tarpaper Shack, in some Slum, and have my Freedom to "VOTE for The GOAT!" (The New Political Party that has Guaranteed Solutions for our Massive Problems!) By The Worldwide People's Revolution!® Book 109, than to be Ordered about like some Dog in some Swanky Army of Voluntary Working Soldiers, who are Paid 60$ per Hour for Setting Marble Tiles on the Solid Stone Walls of their "Beautiful Swanky Stone Dome Home COMPLEXES!" even if they are Rent-free: beCause, I am TERRIFIED by the very Thots of a WICKED One-World Government, which might make a SLAVE of me, just for Rebelling against it. Therefore, I am going to Commit Suicide, before you get Elected by some MOB of Ignorant FOOLS, who do not Realize the Goodness of False Governments, like "The Divided States of United Lies!" (The so-called "United States of North America" in Disguise!) By The Worldwide People's Revolution!® Book 058, which is the Best Government in all of the World, which has only Produced 42 Million Criminals since its Founding in 1776, which only has about 2.2 Million Prisoners, right now, which has gone Down from 2.6 Million, which is quite an Improvement, if you Think about it, and Consider the Fact that Communist Cuba has less than 60,000 Prisoners among 11 Million People. In other Words, not even 0.054% of those Cubans are Criminals, while 40% of Americans are Criminals, who should be Locked Up for Cheating on their Income Taxes; but, the Prisons are already Full. So, what Nazi Concentration Work Camps would we put them into? What they Need is a Good Whipping with a 4-feet by 8-feet Sheet of Plywood. President Trump could handle it.§§

01-15 [_] Well, my Poor Deceived Friend, what they all Desperately Need are LARGE All-Mineral Organic Gardens to Work in, at Home, whereby they can Feed themselves. We Separated 12,000 Wheelbarrows of Topsoil from 6,000 Wheelbarrows of Dirty Rocks, with Picks and Shovels, which any Family could Do, if they had the Land, Freedom, Materials, Money and Tools to do it; but, having a Bad Government, they have been made into SLAVES of Various Kinds. §‡

(WHY Americans, and the Wise People of the Whole World, Want a Righteous KING to Govern them!)

1

01-16 [_] O Selected King, there is no Way in the World that you could ever Persuade Young Men to STOP Eating their Chips and Dips, Drinking Beers, and having Sex Parties with their Painted, Highly-perfumed Skunks: beCause, there is nothing Interesting going on at Swanky Fortresses. §§

01-17 [_] Well, my Sarcastic Friend, you must have not Studied those Drawings very Carefully: beCause, we are Talking about at least a thousand Years of Artistic Work that Needs Doing, unless we Organize **"Seven Great Armies of Working Soldiers!"** Book 015B, like the Beautiful Young Man who is Pictured on the Previous Page, and go about Building those **"GLORIOUS Swanky Hotels Castles and Fortresses!"** as if going to WAR, whereby everyone gets Involved in it, as if we Wanted to Save ourselves from Radical Climate Changes, Unemployment, Suicides, Robberies, the Bug-19, the TERRORISTS, and whomever and whatever might Attack us. For Example, suppose it came a Freezing Rain on all of the Eastern United States during a very Cold Miserable Night, whereby it Rained a Foot or 2 of ICE on every Roof from the Mississippi River to Maine and Florida, whereby they all CAVED-IN — would that get anyone's Attention? For Example, on the next Page you can See what Happened by CHANCE to a large County Storage Shed in Texarkana, Arkansas, when it only Rained Down 4-inches of ICE, and Caved it in! Just Imagine every Roof of every Super Small-mart Store, Target Store, Grocery Store, School, Gymnasium, Bowling Alley, Ball Park, Shopping Mall, Theater, Concert Hall, Church, Gas Station, and House in Eastern United States COLLAPSING! A Foot of Ice will also Cave-in the Roofs of most Vehicles, and the Boxes on Trucks, Trailers, Trains and Airplanes! Almost nothing would be Exempted from the Great Natural DISASTER! Indeed, the Great False Economy would be put into the Trash Dump in just ONE DREADFUL NIGHT! But, you are not Worried about it: beCause, it has not Happened, yet. However, Radical Climate Changes can make it Happen, whenever the Ignorant Fools are not Expecting it, even as they were not Expecting that Ice Storm that Caved-in the Big Tin Roof, which was just one of dozens of Roofs in Texarkana! Moreover, as for that Beautiful Young Man, he would never Touch any Poisonous Drinks, nor Eat any Forbidden Foods: beCause, he Obviously Cares about his Good Health, which is True Wealth, which is True for most Young People, who will be Happy to Eat those Sweet Juicy Fruits and Raw Nuts at Swanky Fortresses, which will be FREE for whomever Wants to Gather them, in Peace! ‡

What country has no jail? ⌃

Netherlands

Surprisingly, **Netherlands** is a country that has no one to put behind the bars. 5 years ago, in 2013, **Netherlands** had 19 prisoners only and now in 2018, this country doesn't have any criminals. May 23, 2018

www.indiatoday.in › gk-current-affairs › story › no-crime...

No crime, no prison! This European country has no criminals to put

Germany has no such thing as federal, state and county facilities. Each state or city **has** its own **prison** and laws. Today Stammheim **has** one institutional manager and three assistant managers. All of them **have** studied law and served as judges. Jan 8, 2018

www.corrections1.com › correctional-healthcare › articles ▾

How the German prison system could guide U.S. prison reform

There are more than **10.35 million people** incarcerated throughout the world with the most being in the United States--more than 2.2 million. Seychelles has the highest prison population rate in the world with 799 per 100,000 of its total population.

1
2
3

4

01-18 [_] O Selected King, here is a Picture of a Secure, Hail-proof, Shingle-proof, Siding-proof, Rot-proof, Paint-proof, Fireproof, Tornado-proof, Insurance-proof Roof, which you Built, which Paid for itself just a Month or so after it was Finished, when a Wicked Tornado Swept over it. †§‡

01-19 [_] Well, my Friend, it only Costed us 2,000$ for the entire 3,000-square-feet of Roof! Therefore, when you Compare that with the normal American Roof, it is not Difficult to Calculate WHO the Ignorant Fools are, who simply Wasted their Time, Money, Materials and Energy! †§‡

1   01-20 [_] O Selected King, when are we going to get around to Discussing **Righteous Anointed Kings versus Powerless Elected Presidents?** Did you Forget the Title of this Chapter, or what?

01-21 [_] Well, my Friend, a Righteous Anointed King, like ME, would Ask for Voluntary Working Soldiers, who would like to Build their own "Beautiful Swanky PALACES!" (A New Concept in Living Habits — Swanky Palaces for Poor People!) By The Worldwide People's Revolution!® Book 066, for themselves and their Families, and then Move into them, Free of all Charges, once they are Finished, and only IF they Promise to do it Correctly, as if Doing it for GOD: beCause, the World has enough Capitalist Trash. So, what would a Powerless President do to Raise your Standard of Living like that? He could Sneeze, Cough in your Face, or even Vomit on you with 250,000 Lies; but, without the Permission of Congress, which is Controlled by Rich Corporations, he could Do nothing Good for anyone, which has been Proven, over and over, during the Past 240 or so Years! Therefore, as God's Anointed Righteous King, I Propose that all of the Tax Slaves should DEMAND: "The GREAT Worldwide TELEVISED Court HEARING!" (That Great Meeting of the Most-Intelligent and Well-Educated Minds!) **By** The Worldwide People's Revolution!® Book 041B, whereby we Slaves might Discover the Whole Truth about each Important Subject. For Example, WHY are there no Criminals in the Netherlands? Why are there no Prisoners over there? Whatever they are Doing, it seems to be Working Riit. Therefore, we all Need to Learn all about it, just in case we Want to Imitate their Plan for True Prosperity. †‡

{That 400-year-old Church is just one Good Example of what everyone could have to Richly Enjoy, if they simply Obeyed their Anointed King, and did with all of their Might whatsoever their Hands Discovered to Do, as the *Holy Bible* Teaches. See *Ecclesiastes.*}

— Chapter 02 —

WHO will Pay for it all?

02-01 [_] If you were to Ask that Question for a Politician to Answer, you would most likely hear him say: "Taxpayers will pay for it": beCause, none of the Politicians have ever Red **"The New MAGNIFIED Version of the 20 Commandments,"** which anyone can Discover in an Inspired Book called: "LIGHTNING STRIKES Versus Lightning Bugs!" (HOW you can Become Moderately RICH, without Telling any Lies nor Selling any Trash!) By The Worldwide People's Revolution!® Book 074, which Reveals that it is the Duty of the Righteous One-World Government to Provide an Unlimited Supply of Good Money, which must be EARNED by Honest Labor, without any Loans, without any Interest, and without any Hateful Taxes: beCause, only Wicked Governments have to Collect Taxes: beCause, everyone within a Righteous Government has Agreed to Learn, Believe, Love, and OBEY those 20 Commandments! Therefore, no Tax Money is Collected for any Reason; but, a Voluntary TITHE is Collected for Operating that Good Government; but, not for Building any Houses, Large Cisterns, Tunnels, Highways, Bridges, Railways, Churches, Mosques, Synagogues, Temples, Cathedrals, Theaters, Gymnasiums, Tennis Courts, Bowling Alleys, Concert Halls, "Royal Swanky Buffets!" (The Best Feasts in the Whole World!) By The Worldwide People's Revolution!® Book 103, nor any Homecraft Workshops with Sales Shops: beCause, all of the Mountains of Rocks are Provided by God, for FREE, along with Mountains of Sand, Gravel, Clay, Rivers of Water, Lakes, Seas, and Oceans. Therefore, the Money is only Needed for HIRING "Seven Great Armies of Working Soldiers!" (HOW to Provide a Way for Everyone to WORK: so as to Eliminate Poverty, Crimes, Drug Abuses, Prisons and Unnecessary Taxes!) By The Worldwide People's Revolution!® Book 015B. †§‡

02-02 [_] O Selected King, why does the *Holy Bible* not just say it Clearly, like you did, whereby any 12-year-old Child might Understand it? The Money is only needed for Paying Wages to Working Soldiers, who can also Plant Trees and Gardens, which will Raise everyone's Standard of Living. After all, when those Working Soldiers get to Liv within "Beautiful Swanky PALACES!" (A New Concept in Living Habits — Swanky Palaces for Poor People!) By The Worldwide People's Revolution!® Book 066, they will not Care whether or not they OWN any such Palaces: beCause they will get to Use them and Enjoy them, which is just as Good as Owning them. Moreover, they will be Able to Save a lot of Money, if they Do a lot of Work: beCause, they will have no Expenses, since their 4 Hours of Common Skilled Labor per Workday will Cover all of their Expenses. Therefore, if they Want to, they can Save ALL of the Money that they Earn by Working any Extra Hours. For Example, after they put in their 4 Hours during the Morning, they can take a 2 Hour Break to Eat Lunch, and Rest until 2 or 3 p.m., and then do another 4 Hours of Work, and put all of that Money into their own Pockets or Safe Deposit Boxes, until they Want to Buy something Special, or take a Swanky Vacation — except that all of those Working Soldiers will have 40 Days of Paid Vacation Time, each Year. Therefore, since all of the Transportation is Free, they can get on a Train, and go wherever they Want to, and Visit any Swanky Fortress in the World, and also Stay there and Work, just as if they were at Home: beCause, the whole Idea is to Keep everyone Healthy and Happy, which does Require some Organizing and Good Management by Well-Educated, Honest, Trustworthy and Reliable People, who Know what they are Doing, who are called "MASTERS," while all of the others are called SERVANTS. Happy Holidays! †‡

1 02-03 [_] Well, my Friend, I am Sure that "The New RIGHTEOUS One-World Government!"
2 can figure out what is Required. Perhaps only 2 Hours of Common Skilled Labor is Required each
3 Day, or the Average thereof. For Example, it might be Possible to Work for 8 Hours on Tuesday,
4 and have the Remainder of the Week Off. For Example, one Man can easily Mop the Floors of 4
5 "Beautiful Swanky Stone Dome Home COMPLEXES!" which will Cover his Expenses:
6 beCause, those Floors will only need to be Mopped once per Week, and only if they are Used. Of
7 course, when the Construction Project is just Begun, all of the Rooms will be Used by the Working
8 Soldiers, which Means that those Floors will need some Mopping and a little Sweeping afterwards.
9

10
11
12 02-04 [_] O Selected King, I would like to Join "The Swanky Associations of Working
13 Soldiers!" (A Fascinating Collection of Various Kinds of Voluntary Working Soldiers!) By
14 The Worldwide People's Revolution!® Book 018B, and particularly **"The Swanky Association
15 of Professional Furniture Makers,"** whereby I can make Fine Hand-crafted Furniture, like that
16 German Desk, which is more than 400 Years Old, which can be Seen in the Marienberg Castle, in
17 Wurzburg, which is a Wonderful Place to Visit, for which a Working Soldier will need some
18 Money, just to Buy the Entrance Ticket: beCause it is not Found in a Swanky Fortress of any Kind.

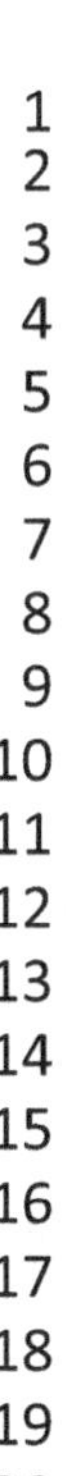

02-05 [_] Well, my Friend, those Working Soldiers will no doubt have Extra Money to Spend on all such Vacations, whereby they will be Able to Afford to give Good Tips, which will keep every Capitalist Slave Extra Happy: beCause most of them are Extremely Poor, and have to Liv in Cramped-up Apartments, or even on River Boats; but, in the United States, they often Liv in Old Rusty Vans, Junked Cars, Abandoned Houses, Under Bridges, and even in Sewage Systems. Therefore, they will all be Happy to Learn about those "Beautiful Swanky PALACES!" which will be Free for all of the Voluntary Working Soldiers, who will not Stop Working on them, until everyone in the Whole World gets to Liv within them, if they Want to. But, no one is going to Twist their Arms, nor FORCE them to Move into them, when they will Cheerfully Do it, and even Defend them with their Lives, once they Discover all of the Benefits — such as Miles and Miles of Fruit Trees, Nut Trees, Grape Vines, Berry Bushes, Vegetable Gardens, and Flower Gardens. ‡

02-06 [_] O Selected King, if you have to Pay 60 Dollars per Hour for a Working Soldier to Install Polished Marble Tiles on his own Solid Stone Walls, in his own Stone Dome Home Complex, it will Cost Billions or Trillions of Dollars to get all of that Work Done Properly. Therefore, how will **"The New RIGHTEOUS One-World Government!"** ever be Able to Afford the Cost of it?

02-07 [_] Well, my Friend, you can only Earn Money, after you have put in your 4 Hours of Common Skilled Labor; and not very many Working Soldiers will be Doing that: beCause, 4 Hours per Workday will Cover all of their Expenses, which will give to them the Remainder of the Day to Play Games, Watch TV, go to Church Services, Theaters, Ball Games, or Reed Good Books. But, no matter what they Do, they must get LOTS of Sleep, whereby they are Well-Rested and Ready for the next 4 Hours of Work the next Day: beCause, we Want everyone to be Healthy and

Happy, which is WHY they are Called WORKING Soldiers. Therefore, if they are not Well-Rested and Doing a Good Job of whatever they are Asked to Do, they will not be Hired to Do any Extra Work: beCause, they are not Qualified for it. Therefore, most of the Work will get Done without any Wages, you might say: beCause, their 4 Hours of Work will Cover all of their Expenses, and all of the Stone Walls will eventually be Covered with Polished Marble Tiles, Ceramic Tiles, or Granite Tiles, and everyone will be Happy with that Plan: beCause, Wages are not really Needed for True Prosperity in such an Economic System as I Propose, even if those Working Soldiers Want Cold Beers to Drink after Working, which they can get at those "Royal Swanky Buffets!" which will Naturally be Discouraged: beCause Alcoholic Beverages are Poisonous; but, Fresh Living Fruit Juices are not Poisonous, if the Fruits have been Grown Correctly; and any of those Juices will be Far Superior to any Stinking Poisonous Beers. Therefore, if you are Tempted to Drink Alcohol, you only need to Replace it with something that is Truly Delicious and Satisfying.

02-08 [_] Most People do not Know it, even as I Lived for most of my Life, and did not Know it; but, those Wild Mountain Goats are Incredibly STRONG: beCause of Living on Natural Wholesome Diets. For Example, they can LEAP UP by as much as 20 Feet High, from a Standing Point, while People do well to Jump Up by 2 to 3 Feet; and only a few People can Jump Up by 4 to 6 Feet; but, none of them by 20 Feet. You could say that the Goats have the Great Advantage of having 4 Legs to Jump with; but, that is not the Whole Story. They have 4 very Strong Legs to Jump with: beCause, they have not Weakened themselves by Eating nor Drinking any Poisons! ‡

02-09 [_] O Selected King, I Like Alcoholic Drinks, and especially if they are Flavored with Mint and Spices, whereby I cannot Taste the Alcohol; but, I get the Good, Natural Effects of getting

Drunk on it, which you might say is a Sin against my own Body; but, it is none of your Business: beCause, it is only MY Business and MY Body. Moreover, if I get Sclerosis of the Liver, and Die from it, it is Okay with me: beCause, I have had a LOT of FUN, just like Stephen Foster had. †§‡

What causes sclerosis of the liver?

The most common **causes** of **Cirrhosis** are Hepatitis C, Alcohol-related **Liver** Disease, Non-Alcoholic Fatty **Liver** Disease, and Hepatitis B. Many people with **Cirrhosis** have no symptoms in the early stages of the disease. Alcohol remains the second most common **cause** of **liver Cirrhosis** after hepatitis C virus.

liverfoundation.org › for-patients › diseases-of-the-liver

Cirrhosis of the Liver - Definition, Symptoms, Causes, and ...

How long does a person live after being diagnosed with cirrhosis of the liver?

The life expectancy for advanced cirrhosis is 6 months to 2 years depending on complications of cirrhosis, and if no donor is available for liver transplantation The life expectancy for people with cirrhosis and acholic **hepatitis** can be as high as 50%.

www.medicinenet.com › cirrhosis › article

What Is Cirrhosis of the Liver? Symptoms, Treatment, Causes ...

What is the difference between cirrhosis and sclerosis of the liver?

Fibrosis of the **liver** typically refers to **scarring of the liver** that has not become significantly extensive; **sclerosis** or **cirrhosis** refers to a condition where **scarring** is extensive and may be irreversible. Mar 12, 2020

www.alcohol.org › comorbid › fibrosis-sclerosis-liver

Treat Alcoholic Fibrosis & Sclerosis | Excessive Drinking Risks

Can sclerosis of the liver be cured?

The treatment for **cirrhosis** depends on what has caused it. **Cirrhosis** cannot usually be **cured**, but there are ways to manage the symptoms and any complications, and stop the condition getting worse.

www.nhs.uk › conditions › cirrhosis › treatment

Treatment for cirrhosis - NHS

02-10 [_] But, it is not all Bad News for the Dietary Sinner: beCause, the Body has Ways and Means of Cleansing itself with some Assistance, and especially by Fasting and Praying with Weeping and Mourning, just as it is written in the *Holy Bible,* which contains Advanced Nolij. Therefore, do not Mock it: beCause, just a Verse or 2 could Save your Life! I Distinctly Remember a Verse that Saved my Life, which is found in *the Book of Omni,* which reads like this: *"Therefore,*

1   *continue with Fasting and Praying, and Endure unto the End, and so shall you be Saved."* Yes, it
2   Required 314 Days of Fasting and Praying; but, afterwards I was as Strong as Samson, whereby
3   Large Rocks were as light as Little Red Bricks! Here is a Picture of some Rocks that I Moved by
4   Hand, after Fasting. They are still there, at 330 Bradley Chapel Road, near Central, Arkansas. †§‡
5

6
7

What are the symptoms of sclerosis of the liver?

Symptoms

- Fatigue.
- Easily bleeding or bruising.
- **Loss of appetite.**
- Nausea.
- Swelling in your legs, feet or ankles (edema)
- Weight loss.
- Itchy skin.
- Yellow discoloration in the skin and eyes (**jaundice**)

  More items... • Dec 7, 2018

www.mayoclinic.org › symptoms-causes › syc-20351487

Cirrhosis - Symptoms and causes - Mayo Clinic

8

How do I clean my liver?

In most cases, a liver detox involves one or more of the following:

1. taking supplements designed to **flush** toxins out of the **liver**.
2. eating a **liver**-friendly diet.
3. avoiding certain foods.
4. going on a juice fast.
5. cleansing the colon and gut through the use of enemas.

Dec 21, 2017

www.medicalnewstoday.com › articles

Liver cleanse: Does it work? - Medical News Today

What are the 4 stages of liver disease?

Stages of liver failure

- **Inflammation**. In this early stage, the liver is enlarged or inflamed.
- Fibrosis. Scar tissue begins to replace healthy tissue in the inflamed liver.
- Cirrhosis. Severe scarring has built up, making it difficult for the liver to function properly.
- End-stage liver disease (ESLD). ...
- Liver cancer.

Apr 9, 2019

www.healthline.com › health › liver-failure-stages

Stages of Liver Failure: What to Expect, Causes, Symptoms, and

How do cirrhosis patients die?

The main causes of 436 deaths among 532 **patients** with **cirrhosis** followed up for up to 16 years constituted liver failure (24%), liver failure with gastrointestinal bleeding (13%), gastrointestinal bleeding (14%), primary liver cell carcinoma (4%), other liver-related causes (2%), infections (7%), cardiovascular ...

pubmed.ncbi.nlm.nih.gov › ...

Main causes of death in cirrhosis - PubMed

Can you live 20 years with cirrhosis?

Class A offers the best prognosis for **cirrhosis** patients with a life expectancy about 15 to **20 years**. Class B is still good with a life expectancy of about 6 to 10 **years**. Thus, there is an ample time for these patients to seek advanced treatment options such as liver transplant. Dec 26, 2018

— Chapter 03 —

"He had a Hell of a LOT of FUN!"

03-01 [_] Actually, in Reality, the Poor Man Suffered during his entire Life with Various Ailments, Itching, Headaches, Legaches, Sore Muscles, Back Pains, Fevers, Colds, Flus, Diarrheas, and you Name it; but, he was very Funny, as if Joking might Camouflage his Ailments, and Hide his Endless Sufferings. He could not See nor Hear very Well, and probably could not Taste Foods nor Drinks very Well. He continually got Worse and WORSE, until he finally Died and went to Hell, while Cursing God and Humanity: beCause he was made Bitter by his Rebellion. Of course, he Tried to Change his Ways; but, not According to God's Plan, whereby he might have been Saved.

03-02 [_] O Selected King, was his Name DAVID? Was he a Distant Relative of King David? How could a Person allow himself to get into such a Hellish Condition? Moreover, he is just one of Millions, who would have to Discipline himself a LOT, just to Save his Soul from all of his Miseries; but, maybe he does not Want to be Saved from it? Maybe he is Happy with himself? §‡

03-03 [_] Well, my Friend, I am Sure that many People are much more Miserable than we can Imagine, who are Unlikely to Confess it: beCause of being Ashamed of themselves; but, we can Set a Good Example for them to Follow, if they Change their Minds, which is what a Swanky Fortress can also do for them, if they ever get Sick of their Vain Traditions. For Example, the Man in the Picture above could Eat mostly Raw Whole Foods, until he Loses his Appetite; and then he could Fast on nothing but Water for 30 to 50 Days, while taking Periodic Enemas with Water, just to Remove some of the Accumulated Slimy Stinking Filth within his Bowels, which would make the Fasting Bearable. But, no matter what, he should Try to Follow *"The Proper RULES for FASTING!" (The Complete Instruction Manual for True Repentance!) By The Worldwide People's Revolution!®* Book 046, lest he should Kill himself by doing it WRong, as some have.

03-04 [_] O Selected King, he had a Hell of a LOT of FUN when he was Young; but, it Backfired on him, and Rewarded him Unjustly, I would say: beCause, he never Really got to Enjoy LIFE. In Fact, if you Counted his "Bad Days," they no doubt Outnumbered his "Good Days," 10 to 1: beCause of his PAINS, as a Result of Playing Football, whereby he Obtained Injuries, and especially Head and Knee Injuries. The Brain Damages Caused other Problems, which are just now being Recognized by Medical Science, which Denied it for 50 or more Years; but, now it is Commonly known to be a BAD Thing for Young Men to Play Football, which is America's Favorite Sport, which used to be Baseball or Basketball. All of them can be Deadly Dangerous! ‡

American football is the most popular sport to watch in the United States, followed by baseball, basketball, and ice hockey, which makes up the "4 major sports".

en.wikipedia.org › wiki › Sports_in_the_United_States

Sports in the United States - Wikipedia

What is the #1 sport in the world?

Soccer

1. **Soccer / Association Football** - 3.5 billion fans. At the top of the list of Most Popular Sports is **soccer** with 3.3-3.5 billion fans all over the world. Oct 3, 2020

sportsshow.net › top-10-most-popular-sports-in-the-world

Top 10 Most Popular Sports in The World - Sports Show

What is America's second favorite sport?

Baseball

Baseball (MLB)

Baseball is **the 2nd most popular sport** in **America** and the 7th **most popular sport** in the world. This **sport** is also known as the United State's national pastime. In **America**, there are mainly two levels of baseball competition, minor league baseball, and major league baseball (MLB). Oct 4, 2020

sportsshow.net › Sports Facts and Trivia

Top 10 Most Popular Sports in America 2020 (TV Ratings ...

03-05 [_] So, it was Capitalism that Drove the Sports into Popularity, and made them what they are, Today: beCause, Money and Power Begets more Money and Power, right? Is that Good? †§‡

Why is the NFL the most popular sport in America?

Two-thirds of all **NFL** money comes from television contracts. That money is distributed 100 percent equally amongst all teams in the league. ... Revenue sharing, salary caps and the vision of a few men many years ago has made the **NFL** head and shoulders above any other **sport in America** in terms of **popularity**.

bleacherreport.com › articles › 11481-why-the-nfl-is-the-...

Why the NFL is the Most Popular Sport in America | Bleacher

What is the hardest sport physically?

Degree of Difficulty: Sport Rankings

SPORT	END	RANK
Boxing	8.63	1
Ice Hockey	7.25	2
Football	5.38	3

33 more rows

www.espn.com › espn › page2 › sportSkills

Page 2 - Sport Skills Difficulty Rankings - ESPN.com

It is not surprising that **basketball** is the world's highest paid sport. As well as earning millions per year in salary, the NBA's best **basketball** players earn a huge amount of money from their various endorsements and sponsorships, more so than any other sport.

www.rulesofsport.com › faq › what-is-the-highest-paid-sp...

What is the Highest Paid Sport in the World? | FAQ | Rules of Sport

Golf holds a long lead over the next most boring sports. American Football is the second most snooze-worthy sport, being branded boring by 59% of people who have ever watched it, followed closely by **cricket** (58%), darts (also 58%) and **snooker** (57%). Jan 10, 2018

yougov.co.uk › sport › articles-reports › 2018/01/10 › w...

What is the most boring sport? | YouGov

03-06 [_] So, why would People Waste their Time and Money on Foolish Sports? Is it beCause they are Spiritually DEAD, or what? Could they not Entertain their Minds by Reading Good Books? I have no Use for Sports, at all, except to Watch the Olympic Gymnastics, or Acrobats. †‡

11 Least Popular Sports in the World

1. 1 | **Kabbadi**. **Kabbadi** is the national sport of Bangladesh and, from what I can tell, it's a mix of rugby without a ball and red rover.
2. 2 | Motocross/motorcycle racing. ...
3. 3 | **Fencing**. ...
4. 4 | Polo. ...
5. 5 | **Archery**. ...
6. 6 | Sailing. ...
7. 7 | Canadian football. ...
8. 8 | Weightlifting. ...

More items... • Jun 13, 2014

11points.com › 11-least-popular-sports-world

11 Least Popular Sports in the World - 11 Points

There's a new sport in town, and it looks like it's here to stay! **Pickleball** is currently the fastest growing sport in the world and there's no question why — it's fun, a great workout and almost anyone can pick it up quickly. It's also super inexpensive to maintain and requires very little skill to get involved. Oct 10, 2019

www.dailycal.org › 2019/10/10 › pickleball-worlds-fastes...

Pickleball: World's fastest growing sport that no one has ever heard of

It's been a long time coming, but it might be time to finally make it official: The **NBA** has surpassed **MLB** as America's second-biggest sports league. ... For the first time ever, the average value of an **NBA** team ($1.9 Billion) is worth more **than** the average value of an **MLB** team ($1.7 Billion), according to Forbes. Apr 11, 2019

sports.yahoo.com › mlb-nba-team-values-lebron-james-m...

NBA teams pass MLB in average value, per Forbes - Yahoo! Sports

Why is America so good at sports?

America has dedicated coaches, and offers several opportunities to compete and/or train for a sport. **America** also has an organized system, and unlike some of the countries in the world, **America** encourages children to play **sports**.

www.quora.com › Why-is-America-so-good-at-sports

Why is America so good at sports? - Quora

03-07 [_] O Selected King, how about some Rich Person, like you, offering a Million Dollars for whomever does enough Fasting and Praying to get the Power of God for Doing Miracles, whereby we could get some Competition in the Sport of FASTING? Would that not Prove to be Interesting?

1 03-08 [_] Yes, my Friend, that would Prove to be very Interesting — except that God might not
2 be Interested in it: beCause it is like putting a Price on Gifts from God, which is something that
3 Oral and Richard Roberts might Like; but, God would Naturally Hate it: beCause, it is like Selling
4 Sunshine and Rainwater to Poor People in Thirsty Deserts, who should be Assisted by a Righteous
5 Government to Build Large Swanky Cisterns for Water Storage, which Water can be Shipped in
6 from the Amazon River, where it is now just Running Away into the Atlantic Ocean, and does not
7 Benefit anyone, which Reminds me of the Vietnam War, when Americans Dumped more Tons of
8 Bombs on Cambodia, than they Dumped on Japan during the Second World War: beCause, the
9 Federal Fake Government of "The Divided States of United Lies!" (The so-called "United
10 States of North America" in Disguise!) By The Worldwide People's Revolution!® Book 058,
11 has Money to Waste on War Games; but, no Money to Help Poor People — such as those Poor
12 Refugees, who Fled to Thailand for Help, and got Trucked Back to Cambodia, and Murdered:
13 beCause, the United States did not Want to Help Feed them, even though it was the United States
14 that made them into Refugees in a "round about way," just like they made tens of millions of
15 Refugees in Afghanistan, Iraq, Syria, Somalia, Sudan, Libya, Ethiopia, Egypt, Palestine, Cuba,
16 Venezuela, Colombia, Ecuador, Bolivia, and wherever: beCause, that is the Nature of Capitalism!
17

18

A **refugee** has a well-founded fear of persecution for reasons of race, religion, nationality, political opinion or membership in a particular social group. Most likely, they cannot return home or are afraid to do so. War and ethnic, tribal and religious violence are leading **causes** of **refugees** fleeing their countries.

www.unrefugees.org › refugee-facts › what-is-a-refugee

What is a Refugee? Definition and Meaning | USA for UNHCR

en.wikipedia.org › wiki › Refugee_crisis ▾

Refugee crisis - Wikipedia

Jump to Preventing the root **causes** of migration — Causes for the crisis of the refugees can include war and civil war, human rights violations, environment ...

Middle East and North Africa: 2.739 million   Europe: 4.391 million

Africa: 4.413 million   Asia and the Pacific: 3.831 million

Causes · Political responses · Migratory routes and ... · Modern and ...

19
20 03-09 [_] Like most Problems in this World of Woes, the Refugee Problem is no Problem, until
21 YOU become a Refugee, yourself, who has been Displaced from your Homeland, who now finds
22 yourself in a Foreign Land, among Strangers who Hate you for the Color of your Skin, the Size of
23 your Tally Whacker, the Shape of your Nose, Language, Accent, Habits, Traditions, Clothing,
24 Poverty, or whatever Faults that they Discover with you. Yes, it is somewhat like my Inspired
25 Books, which are Rejected by Ignorant People, who say: "I do not like the way he capitalizes so
26 many of his meaningless words — such as love and hate, which have only one definition, which I
27 cannot remember." However, the Swanky Fortress System will Eliminate that Refugee Problem
28 by Helping all Groups of People to Prosper, at Home, in their own Countries, or wherever they are
29 Welcome, even if they are Extremely Stupid People, who must be Assisted by Compassionate
30 People with Good Understanding, who See them as being Valuable to Humanity in some Way. †‡
31
32 03-10 [_] O Selected King, this is one very Sad World that we Liv in, which has Surely Suffered
33 Long Enough, and is now Ready for a Brand-New Lifestyle within those **"GLORIOUS Swanky**

Hotels Castles and Fortresses!" (Beautiful Planned City States for WISE Intelligent Well-Educated People with Common Sense and Good Understanding!) By The Worldwide People's Revolution!® Book 019B. For Example, the Poor Abused People in Central America should be Assisted to Build their own Beautiful Planned City States, who can be Trained by the United States Army Engineers, who can have Mercy on them. Otherwise, they can be Helped by the Peace Corps. {Better yet, my Friend, they should Study: "A Sound Argument for Good Masters and Obedient Servants!" (WHY Everyone Needs a Good Master, and every Master Needs Good Obedient Servants!) By The Worldwide People's Revolution!® Book 008B. †‡}

www.peacecorps.gov › about ▾

About - Peace Corps

The Peace Corps is a service opportunity for motivated changemakers to immerse themselves in a community abroad, working side by side with local leaders to tackle the most pressing challenges of our generation.

Agency Jobs · History · Global Initiatives · Leadership

Do you get paid in the Peace Corps?

Peace Corps provides a number of benefits that **make** the Volunteer experience almost free: flights to and from your country of service, full medical and dental coverage, a monthly living stipend, housing, technical and language training, and a readjustment allowance when **you** finish, just to name just a few perks. May 1, 2020

www.peacecorps.gov › stories › how-much-does-peace-c…

How much does Peace Corps cost?

How do you get into the Peace Corps?

Seven Steps to get Accepted into the Peace Corps

1. **Join the Peace Corps** Prep Program. …
2. Take some language classes. …
3. Seek out intercultural experiences. …
4. Choose your sector focus and get experienced. …
5. Give back and volunteer. …
6. Meet with a recruiter. …
7. Do NOT apply to a position you are not qualified for.

career.asu.edu › seven-steps-get-accepted-peace-corps

Seven Steps to get Accepted into the Peace Corps | Career and …

Incidents of physical and sexual assault do occur, although most Volunteers complete their two years of service without a serious safety and security incident. Together, the **Peace Corps** and Volunteers can reduce risk, but cannot truly eliminate all risk. Read more on how the **Peace Corps** approaches Safety and Security.

www.peacecorps.gov › ghana › preparing-to-volunteer

Safety and Security - Peace Corps

Can you get laid in the Peace Corps?

Bottom line, **if you** want to **have sex**, it is available. **Peace Corps** volunteers are typically young, healthy, and mixed gender. **I do** not think there is a force in the world that **would** stop all of them from having **sex**, given the length of their stay.

www.quora.com › Does-joining-the-Peace-Corps-pretty-…

Does joining the Peace Corps pretty much mean you most likely will …

Is Peace Corps hard to get into?

Last year, the **Peace Corps** received more than 17,000 applications for fewer than 4,000 positions. … Serving as a **Peace Corps** Volunteer is a professional opportunity with lifelong benefits, so it is extremely competitive. If you think you **have** what it takes to compete, apply here. Ready to start your **Peace Corps** journey? May 6, 2015

www.peacecorps.gov › stories › how-competitive-is-the-p…

How competitive is the Peace Corps?

03-11 [_] Unlike the Peace Corps, anyone can get into a Swanky Army of Working Soldiers, even if they cannot Reed nor Riit. In Fact, they can get into a Swanky Army of Working Soldiers, if they only know how to have Sex, and nothing more: beCause they can be Tawt whatever else they Need to Learn — such as how to Shovel Sand and Gravel into a Concrete Mixing Machine, which might Require all of 10 to 15 Minutes to Learn, unless they are Extremely Stupid, in which Case they can be Trained to Hoe Weeds, Pick Fruits, Mop Floors, Peel Carrots, Wash Dishes, Sweep Out Trains, or do some other Useful Work. Indeed, at the very least, they can Entertain the People who want to make Fun of them, and be Tawt how to Enjoy that Mistreatment, and be Rewarded for Accepting it, until they can Find their Rightful Place within the Swanky Fortress System. Most likely, they just Need someone to LOVE, who also Loves them. Therefore, they can be Tawt HOW to Love other People, and HOW to get other People to Love them, which might Require a Day or 3; but, once they Learn it, they will Fit right into the System, and get to Enjoy their own "Beautiful Swanky PALACES!" (A New Concept in Living Habits — Swanky Palaces for Poor People!) By The Worldwide People's Revolution!® Book 066. One of the First Things that they will have to Do, is to Fill Out and File "The Complete SURVEYS of our VALUES!" (SURVEYS of Religious Spiritual Political Governmental Sexual Social Moral Economical Business Labor Habitual and Miscellaneous VALUES!) By The Worldwide People's Revolution!® Book 059, or at least "The Simplistic SURVEYS of our VALUES!" Book 059B, whereby "The New RIGHTEOUS One-World Government!" Book 056, can Obtain some Idea concerning WHO they are Dealing with, and what their Degree of Intelligence might be: beCause, some of them will no doubt Qualify to become Leaders and Masters of Special Crafts, who will be Assisted and Promoted in the System, just as long as they are Trying Hard to Do a GOOD JOB of whatever they Do, while also Learning whatever Truths that they can Learn in all Good Books, and especially in Inspired Books, like mine, which some People will Naturally say are NOT Inspired by any Loving Godly God. However, we can Prove that they are Inspired by some God: beCause, you or anyone else, can Experiment with the following Test:

A-[_] Just pick up any given Book, and Open it at Random to any Page, and Reed the first Words that your Eyes land on, and See for yourself if it Speaks to your Heart. If it does not, it is the WRong Book. Therefore, pick up another Book, and Test it. (I just now Tested such a Book, and just Happened to Discover the very Answer to my own Personal Question, which "Hit the Nail on the Head," as they say. It Works for me every Time! †§‡)

B-[_] I Believe that it might Work for me, if I just have Faith in it; but, I do not have any Faith in Uninspired books, which are not even Capitalized. For Example, Jesus wrote a Book, called: *The Light of the World,* which was never Published: beCause, no one Believed it enough to Publish it; but, someone else took up the Idea a couple thousand Years later, and made it Successful, and Sold a Billion Copies of it to Santa Claus. †§‡§§

C-[_] I Confess that God could Direct a Person's Eyeballs to the Exact Riit Words that such a Person Needs to Learn, if God Wants to; but, he might have to Love us, first; and it is sometimes Difficult to Love People, and especially if they are simply not Lovable. †§‡

D-[_] Democrats are not very Lovable; but, I can Love some Republicans, and especially Independent Jackasses, if they have Big Chime Bells to Ring, if you know what I Mean. §

E-[_] Educated People might Guess what you Mean; but, not everyone is Turned On by SEX: beCause their Minds are not Inside of the Pants of everyone on the Street; but, if they See any Naked Legs, they might get Interested in other Body Parts, if they are Young and Healthy. Therefore, the Key to being Loved, is to be Young and Healthy, even if you ain't.

F-[_] I Fail to Understand what this Survey is all about. Can anyone Enlighten my Mind?

G-[_] God Knows that you are not too Bright-minded. Therefore, just Skip over it. Move.

H-[_] I Honestly Think that the Author is a bit Crazy; but, not in a Bad Way. If he Wants to Join the Peace Corps, let him Join; but, I am going to Steer Clear of it: beCause I have no Desire to be an Underpaid Slave of any Kind. Indeed, I Want Good Swanky Wages all of the Time, even to Hoe my own Weeds in my own Garden: beCause, I cannot Tolerate the Idea of doing any Work for NOTHING: beCause, I Like what Money will Buy, in spite of the Fact that it cannot Buy a Beautiful Sunrise, nor Sunset. In Fact, it cannot Buy any Really GOOD Things: beCause, none of those Things are Found for Sale! Otherwise, Rich People, like Medical Doctors and Lying Lawyers, might have Good Health; but, it is not Found for Sale in any Grocery Stores, which is Obtained by Eating Natural Wholesome Foods, which must be Grown and Eaten at HOME: beCause, just 10 Minutes after Harvesting most Vegetables, they have Lost half of their Vitamins! And then, one Day Later, they are not Fit to Eat for Vitamin C, for Example: beCause it has Evaporated. †§‡

I-[_] Innocent Children can Grow Up on nothing but Mother's Breast Milk and Ripe Bananas with a few Raisins, until they are 3 to 4 Years Old, and then they can begin to Eat Fresh Raw Greens from the Garden with Steamed Butternut Squashes, and Liv to be 900 Years Old, if their Bodies and Minds are not Polluted with Refined Sugars, Starches, Boiled Oils, and all such Unnatural Things. Indeed, they almost always like a few Fresh Raw Dried NUTS, Tree-ripened Apricots, Peaches, Pears, Apples, Mangos, Cherimoyas, Yellow

Sapotes, Lychees, Rambutans, Immature Coconuts, and other Tropical Fruits; but, you cannot Discover Good Fruits in any Gross Grocery Stores: beCause, most of them are Harvested for Capitalists, who must Profit from Selling them, which Means that they must be Picked Green and Immature, whereby they have more Acids in them, which Destroy a Person's Precious Teeth, if not his Riit Mind. Therefore, it is Dangerous, just to Eat them!

J-[_] Justice Demands that everyone should have a Good Garden of Eden to Eat from, and make Sweet Fruit Juices from Ripe Berries, Cherries, Grapes, and Plums, which will keep the Bowels Working Correctly; but, only IF People Consume Wholesome Natural Foods, and NO Highly-processed JUNK Foods — such as Candy Bars, Iced Creams, Peanut Butter and Jelly Sandwiches, Cookies, Cakes, Pastries, Puddings, Syrups, Refined Flours, nor any of those Goodies: beCause, they are all Forbidden Foods, including French-fried Foods: beCause, Boiled Oils are Abominations within Human Bodies. Therefore, *"Straat and Narrow is the Way that Leads to Everlasting Good Health, and few are the People who Discover it: beCause, Wide and Broad is the Way that Leads to Self-Destruction, and many are the Masses of Ignorant People who Fall Headlong into those Eating Pits along the Polluted Streets of Sin City,"* as Jesus might say. Therefore, if anyone Wants True Justice, they will have to DEMAND: "The GREAT Worldwide TELEVISED Court HEARING!" (That Great Meeting of the Most-Intelligent and Well-Educated Minds!) **By The Worldwide People's Revolution!®** Book 041B, whereby they might Learn the WHOLE Truth about each Important Subject, including our Dietary Sins. †§‡§§

K-[_] King Jesus would say to Eat whatever is Sold in the Market Places, asking no Questions for Conscience' Sake: beCause, it is not that which Enters into our Mouths that Defiles us as much as that which comes Out of our Mouths from our Unclean Minds, which are Perverted by our Unclean Foods, which Accumulate within our Bowels, which are Full of Ancient Morbid Putrid Matter, which anyone can Smell in Restrooms, which STINK. Therefore, *Stop Thinking Evil, and you will soon have a Natural Appetite to Eat Good Sweet Fruits from the Tree of Life.* But, if you Think Evil, you will soon have an Unnatural Appetite to Eat with the Hogs and Dogs, which can easily be Proven in a Courtroom, which has already been Proven in Courtrooms a million Times over: beCause, if we Lust after Forbidden Things, we will Obtain them, unto our own Great Shame, even as the Adulterer has already Testified, who should have been Contented with his own Wife, and she with her own Husband: beCause Adultery and Fornication are only for Ignorant Fools, whose Minds are Spiritually Blinded to the Greater Truths, which are also the Greater Riches and more Pleasant, Heavenly Pleasures, which come with Peace of Mind and Contentment. †‡

L-[_] Lots of Laughs! King Jesus never even got to Experience the Great Pleasures of having Frot Sex, whereby he Missed Out on the Best Sex there is, which was Discovered by the Ancient Greeks, whom God Blessed for Practicing FIDELITY: beCause, he Loves Fidelity above all Things, which is WHY that he Blest King David and his Lover called Jonathan: beCause, they were Men after God's own Heart and Mind. Therefore, King David will Arise Again, to Govern all of Israel, who will be Practicing Frot Sex, even as Jacob and Jehovah God were Practicing it at the Brook called PENIEL, or Penuel, from which Root Word PENIS is Derived: beCause, that is how Jehovah God has Survived for Billions of Years without having Sexual Intercourse with any Wombman. (See *Genesis*

32.) Yes, it is a very Curious Subject, which needs to be Addressed at **"The GWTCH!"** Book 041B: beCause, it Reveals HOW TO LIV FOREVER IN A STEADY STATE OF HEAVENLY BLISS! Yes, LOVE is the Principle Thing, O Mockingbirds. So, get on it. §

M-[_] I say that MONEY is the Principle Thing: beCause, what can a Person Do without Money to Work with? Yes, to Hell with Unsafe Sex and Vain Pleasures, which Money might Buy; but, it cannot Buy Good Sex: beCause, in Order to have Good Sex, one must have Good Health; and, in Order to Obtain Good Health, one must have LOTS of MONEY, whereby he can Buy his own "Beautiful Swanky PALACES!" Book 066, and get himself into Good Mental, Spiritual, and Physical Shape, whereby he can Liv Forever! But, that is not to say that a Person should be a Fool, and make a Slave of himself, just to Obtain more Money, when it is the DUTY of **"The New RIGHTEOUS One-World Government!"** to Mint and Print the Necessary New Money — NOT to give it away to Beggars, nor to Waste it on Rich Edomite Bankers; but, in Order to Use that New Money WISELY, in Order to HIRE **"Seven Great Armies of Working Soldiers!" (HOW to Provide a Way for Everyone to WORK: so as to Eliminate Poverty, Crimes, Drug Abuses, Prisons and Unnecessary Taxes!) By The Worldwide People's Revolution!®** Book 015B, in Order to Build those **"GLORIOUS Swanky Hotels Castles and Fortresses!" (Beautiful Planned City States for WISE Intelligent Well-Educated People with Common Sense and Good Understanding!) By The Worldwide People's Revolution!®** Book 019B! §‡

N-[_] Not every Nitwit can Understand such a Statement of Facts; but, it is True that everyone could be Moderately RICH, without Telling any Lies, nor Selling any Capitalist Trash: beCause, it does not Require a College Diploma to Mix Up Concrete, nor to Lay Cut Stones on a Wall; but, it only Requires some MUSCLES and Common Sense, which any Workhorse just Naturally has. Therefore, why should such a Workhorse make a Lifetime Slave of himself, just to EAT and Sleep in a Barn? Why not Do a Moderate Amount of Work, every Workday, and Liv in a Swanky PALACE? And in the Meantime, those Working Soldiers can still Attend Classes in Schools, whereby they can Learn all Kinds of Special Crafts and Needed Skills: beCause, there are Swanky CASTLES to be Built, which will Need the Best of our ARTS and Crafts, just to be Inviting all Kinds of Visitors, who will be Coming for many Ages to Come, just to See those Glorious Castles!

O-[_] Are there no Options to Choose from, O King David? Must we all Humbly Submit to **"The Swanky Sword of Divine Truths!" (The Most-Powerful Weapon in the Whole Universe!) By The Worldwide People's Revolution!®** Book 067, and do our Best to Please our Anointed KING, who would have all of us become Moderately RICH, like the Young Man who is Shown on the next Page, who is Healthy, Wealthy, and WISE, like me?

P-[_] People like him should be Mounted in Museums, in Marble Statues, for everyone to Richly Enjoy, like Michelangelo's David, who only needed a larger and longer Tally Whacker to Play with, since his Chime Bells are just Riit, and his Muscles are Perfect. I would be very Happy to Join any Disciplined Army of Working Soldiers, who are Composed of Beautiful Young Men like him, just as long as one of them would Agree to Love me, and Practice FIDELITY with me: beCause, that is the Principle Thing with God. ‡§‡

1
2

1
2
3   Q-[_] Saint Dan is more Beautiful, in my Honest Opinion; but, I Love all of them. The
4   Great Question is this, "How will we ever get to Richly Enjoy all of the Beautiful Young
5   People, if they have Committed Suicide for a Lack of HOPE in the Future, whereby they
6   have something Good to Look Forward to, and Hope in?" Answer that Question, first. †§‡

1

R-[ ] He is a Registered Pure-Breed Mustang, you might say, whose Muscles only need to be Harnessed, and put to Work Laying Heavy Cut Stones on a Swanky Fortress Wall, whereby he can Look Back at the End of the Day, and See his Great Accomplishments, which he cannot Do by Lifting Weights: beCause, other than his Beautiful Muscles, he has nothing to Show for all of that Sweat! Therefore, what he Desperately Needs is "The New RIGHTEOUS One-World Government!" which will not be making a Slave of him, nor of anyone else: beCause, it will Reward all such Good People with those "Beautiful Swanky PALACES!" (A New Concept in Living Habits — Swanky Palaces for Poor People!) By The Worldwide People's Revolution!® Book 066. Yes, it is a Fair Exchange in the Mind of any Honest Businessman. But, if you Doubt it, just Ask them at: "The GREAT Worldwide TELEVISED Court HEARING!" Book 041B. Indeed, I Dare say that not one Man will Stand Up and Say that it is Unfair, which is Equally as Good for the Ladies, as it is for the Gentlemen, who will be Happy to Build those Swanky Palaces for their Ladies to Richly Enjoy, who can also Contribute their Fair Share of the Work by Making the Uniforms, and Preparing the Meals and Clean Beds for those Working Soldiers that they Love. But, if they are Pregnant, and Want to Rest, that is Okay, let them Rest in Peace and Enjoy the Beautiful Scenery around Swanky Hotels, which will be Flowery. †§‡

S-[ ] O Selected King, if I want to Look at Beautiful Naked Young Men, I just go to the Gym, and wait around in the Shower Room, until they come in; and sometimes they come in a half-dozen at a Time: beCause, it is Obvious what they Want, and it is NOT Ancient Clean Greek Frot Sex; but, it is SODOMY, which is Nasty, Filthy, Stinking, Dangerous, Disease-spreading, Disgusting, Demeaning, Dehumanizing, Degrading, Demoralizing, and Effeminizing, while Clean Frot Sex is Perfectly Natural for Young Men, according to www.Man2ManAlliance.org which is the Official Authority on that Subject, which no one has Proven to be WRong by any Means. Even Jesus Practiced it, and so did Saint Paul. †§‡

T-[ ] Well, my Friend, it is something that should be Proven at **"The GWTCH,"** after the more-Important Subjects are Addressed: beCause, it is not like a Viirus that has gotten Out of Control; but, Sexual Acts are still very Important Issues: beCause a lot of Sex Crimes are Committed beCause of Extra-Horny Men, which was made known by the Boy Scout Masters, Catholic Priests, Medical Perverts, and whomever. For Example, an Average of 3,000 Teenage Boys are Murdered, each Year, in Houston, Texas, alone, after making "Unholy Connections" with Judges, Lawyers, Policemen, Politicians, and even Preachers and Teachers, who Murdered their Victims, just to make Sure that they did not Tell on them for their Forbidden and Illegal Acts. Just Imagine that! First they Abuse them, Use them, and then Murder them for Selfish Reasons, which would never Happen at any Swanky Fortresses: beCause, there would be no Poor Desperate Young Men, looking for Money to Liv on: beCause, they could all go to those "Royal Swanky Buffets!" (The Best Feasts in the Whole World!) By The Worldwide People's Revolution!® Book 103, to Eat, in Exchange for a little Work. Therefore, they would not have to Prostitute themselves for getting enough Money to Stay in School, Buy some Clothes, nor Help their Mothers. ‡

U-[ ] I Understand that we Americans have some MASSIVE Problems; but, none of those Problems will be Solved by Building Swanky Fortresses: beCause they will be Full of Drug Addicts, Sex Perverts, Gluttons, Drunkards, Unemployed Sloths, and the Lowest of the Low Classes of People: beCause, all of the Good, Honest, Hardworking People will just

Naturally be WORKING: beCause, like me, they are Presently Working. Therefore, those Swanky Fortresses will be Filled with the Dross, Scum and Low Life of Society, you might say, who have been made that Way by the Lust for more Money, called Capitalism. †§‡§§

V-[_] Queen Victoria might Disagree with thee: beCause the Good People will Naturally Learn about Swanky Fortresses, and Visualize them as Good Things, and thus, FLEE from all Cities of Confusion, and Happily Join those Swanky Associations of Working Soldiers.

W-[_] I would rather Die in a Hateful WAR, than Submit to "The Swanky Sword of Divine Truths!" which has no Right to Dominate over me: beCause, "I did NOT Vote!" (There are 7 Billion Reasons!) **By The Worldwide People's Revolution!**® Book 138. §

X-[_] X-number of People are General Boneheads, who cannot be Tawt anything that they Need to Learn: beCause, they have never been Hungry Enough to make their Brains Work Correctly, which Requires some Fasting, Praying, Mourning, and Confessing their Sins, which is a Guaranteed Solution for that Problem. {See: "A Sound Argument for Good Masters and Obedient Servants!" (WHY Everyone Needs a Good Master, and every Master Needs Good Obedient Servants!) By The Worldwide People's Revolution!® Book 008B, which Totally Eliminates the Bonehead, Dimwit Problem in Short Order! †§}

Y-[_] I am Yearning to Learn what Ails me, and how to Correct it. Where can I Learn it?

Z-[_] The Great Zeal of our Selected King will make that Possible. Have Faith, O Sinner.

03-12 [_] O Selected King, even King David would find it Difficult to Straighten Out the American Disorderly Disaster: beCause, it is Extremely Complicated. For Example, the President can give a Speech, and perhaps only 20 to 30 percent of the People even Listen to it, while the others are Engaged in Sex Orgies, Consuming Drugs, Eating at Buffets, getting Drunk, Playing Ball Games, or doing whatever they are Doing: because, no one can even get their Attention, including yourself.

03-13 [_] Well, my Friend, I must Confess that it is a Big MESS; but, God has the Best Solution, which is to STOP the Rain, Dry Up the Fields, Burn Down the Forests, and Choke everyone to Death on the SMOKE! However, not even that will get their Attention Turned toward Provable Truths, whereby they might Learn a few Important Things: beCause, they are Drugged Out of their Riit Minds. Therefore, I might as well Talk to a Tree, or to a Rock: beCause, they are Spiritually Dead People, who have no Idea what Great and Wonderful Pleasures that they are Missing! †§‡§§

03-14 [_] O Selected King, a certain Percentage of the People still have their Riit Minds, whom you must Contact, somehow, and get them to Help you. Indeed, all that you Need is some Money to Hire them to Build the First Glorious Swanky Hotel, Castle and Fortress, which will soon be Supporting itself, by Means of those Wind Generators on the Great Plains: beCause, the Wind is Blowing over there for most of the Time, and about 12 to 20 Miles per Hour. Therefore, you can Capture it, and Transform it into ElecTrickery. (See the Special Drawings above Verse 01-12.) †‡

— Chapter 04 —

Putting the Wind to Work for us!

04-01 [_] O King David, the Wind is Unreliable, and might be Blowing this Way for a Minute, and suddenly Turn about and Blow the other Way for 10 Minutes, and then Stop. Therefore, just as soon as the Turbine gets to Spinning Good, the Wind Changes Directions. Therefore, beCause Swanky Fortresses do not Spin around and Face the Wind, Directly: beCause of being Permanent Stone Walls with Fixed Wind Generators, most of the Wind-Power is Lost. However, if there are Large Swanky Wind-Generators on ALL SIDES of the Fortress, and at the Tops of each of the Stone Terraces, there will always be Turbines Turning, if the Wind is Blowing for more than 10 Minutes. Indeed, it would likely Require 10 Minutes, just to get a Huge Swanky Turbine Turning from a Standing Point: beCause its Weight will Naturally Resist the Wind for a few Minutes, until the Turbine gets to Spinning; and then the LOAD of the Generator will be put on it, which will Naturally Slow it Down a bit, or as much as it might be Engineered to Do, Depending on the Speed of the Wind. For Example, if the Wind is Blowing at 40 Miles per Hour on the 4th Terrace Up, the Turbine will have to be Geared Down, just to Slow it Down, and keep it from Wrecking itself in the Ferocious Wind: beCause, we are Talking about Fins or Sails that are 30 feet Wide on the Axles, which might be 2 feet in Diameter, and have 10 Large Fins on just one Axle, which will Act like Sails in the Wind on a Ship, which will be Designed to Catch the Wind, and make the Axle Spin, Rapidly, which will be Geared to the Electric Generator, which might Produce more ElecTrickery than the Grand Coulee Dam, in just 20 of those Large Swanky Wind Generators! †‡

What city is the Grand Coulee Dam in?   ⌃

Spokane, Washington

Grand Coulee Dam, on the **Columbia River** west of **Spokane, Washington**, is one of the largest structures ever built by mankind--a mass of concrete standing 550 feet high and 5,223 feet long, or just shy of a mile. Jan 13, 2017

www.nps.gov › articles › washington-grand-coulee-dam ▾

Washington: Grand Coulee Dam (U.S. National Park Service)

Which is bigger Grand Coulee or Hoover Dam?   ⌃

Grand Coulee Dam's Size

The **Hoover Dam** is 726 feet tall and is 1,245 feet long, and many lives were lost in the process of it being built. The **Grand Coulee Dam** is 550 feet tall and 5,200 feet long, and it is one of the biggest concrete structures in the world.

prezi.com › grand-coulee-dam-vs-hoover-dam

Grand Coulee Dam VS. Hoover Dam by Grahm Mayers - Prezi

04-02 [_] Now, just Compare those Dams with the Great Stone Terraced Walls around a Glorious Swanky Fortress, which might be 100 Miles Long on just one Side of it, and 10 to 60 Terraces High! Each Great Terrace will Catch the Wind, no matter which Direction it is Blowing from: beCause, the Terrace goes all around the entire Swanky Fortress, which might be a hundred Miles in Diameter! Yes, you might Think that those Tall Stone Walls would STOP the Wind from Blowing; but, it is not True: beCause the Wind picks up Speed on the Flat Plains: beCause, there are no Trees nor Mountains to Stop it. Therefore, if a Swanky Fortress is Built in the Windy Part of the Great State of Flexible Texas, for Example, you can well Believe that those Electric Generators will be Pumping Out Electricity most of the Time, both Day and Night. Moreover, if we have to, we can put the Stone Funnels on Ball Bearings, whereby the Arcades can Face the Wind for most of the Time; but, it is Self-Defeating: beCause, the "Secret" to Catching the Wind is the Tall Stone Wall in front of the Arcade of Wind Generators, which Funnels the Wind into the Arcade of Wind Generators. Therefore, if we need more Powerful Winds, we only need to make those Stone Walls TALLER: beCause, the Strongest Winds are Up in the Sky. Therefore, the Generators at the Top Terraces will Naturally be doing more Work than the Lower Generators. †‡

04-03 [_] O Selected King, there will be a HUGE Amount of STRESS on those Metal Fins, which are likely to WEAR OUT, and have to be Replaced with New Fins; and the Axles will need New Ball Bearings: beCause they will also Wear Out, if they are Worked a lot, as you say. Therefore, I am wondering if those Generators will Prove to be profitable? After all, the Bearings are not Cheap.

04-04 [_] Well, my Friend, your Question is Perfectly Fair — will those Electric Generators be Profitable, and for how Long, before they have to be Replaced? Will such a Generator Cost as much as a single Car? Probably more; but, no more than 10 Cars, and should Endure for 100 or more Years, and Produce 10 Million Dollars-worth of Electricity. However, I Propose that we Construct SMALL Wind Generators for each Swanky Stone Dome Home Complex, which Cost less than one Car per Generator. After all, we will have Millions of Swanky Cisterns for "Batteries" for Storing the Power in the Water: beCause of having all of those Great TERRACES, which make it Possible and Practical. We can also have a Backup System that uses Ox Power and Horse Power on Electric Generators, just in case the Wind is not Blowing enough, or the Sunlight is not Shining enough to Produce HOT SAND, which can be Used for making Steam Power for Driving Pumps.

04-05 [_] O Selected King, the Hot Sand Solution is not as Good as the Hot SALT Solution: beCause, Hot Salt can Retain its Heat 7 Times as Long as Hot Sand; and we have Oceans of Salt to Exploit, which Water can be Distilled, whereby we can Water the Fruit Trees and Gardens, while Saving the Salt in 50-pound Rectangular Blocks, which can be Stacked Up Properly for Absorbing the Heat that comes from Parabolic Mirrors, which are Aimed at Glass Hot Houses with Triple Panes on the Sunny Side. In other Words, the Triple Panes of Glass will Insulate the Solar Hot House with the Salt Blocks, which can be Used Wisely for Heating the Swanky Stone Dome Home Complexes to Consistent Comfortable Temperatures, even if it is Minus 40 °F. †§‡

04-06 [_] Well, my Friend, we will have to Do some Experimenting, just to Discover what Works Best, which will take some TIME; but, in the Meantime, we can be Working on those Great TERRACES, which can be made with HUGE 500,000-gallon Swanky CISTERNS for Water Storage, which must be Lined with Ceramic Tiles, which alone will keep an Army of Working Soldiers very Busy, while their Fruit and Nut Trees are Growing, which will have to be Transplanted into the Great Terraces, once they are Ready for the Trees. Therefore, a lot of

Organizing will be Required by the Generals in Charge of it, who will have to Deal with all Kinds of Enemies — such as Diseases, Insects, Killing Frosts, High Winds, Hailstorms, Droughts, and whatever Satan Throws at us, who is Full of Deceptive Tricks. (See *the Book of Jobe* for the Proof.)

04-07 [_] O Selected King, there must be at least a Million Plant Diseases, and a Billion Kinds of Insects to Deal with; but, when we do our Gardening according to: "The LUSCIOUS All-Mineral Organic Method of Gardening!" (HOW to Grow DELICIOUS Satisfying Foods for Potential Kingz and Kweenz in Beautiful Swanky PALACES!) By The Worldwide People's Revolution!® Book 021B, the Problems are Greatly Reduced: beCause, the Minerals and Organic Matter Greatly Strengthen the Plants, while the Natural Predators take Care of the Unwanted Bugs. Therefore, it is not a Dreadful, nor Frightening Field of Endeavors to get into. For Example, here is a Picture of some of your own Muscat Grapes to Study, which had no Diseases nor Bug Problem.

04-08 [_] Well, my Friend, the Problem there was the Fact that the Buyer of the Property did not Water the Grapes; but, just let them Die; and then he Tore Down the 2,000-dollar Grape Arbor: beCause the Dead Vines looked "Ugly" to him. However, the Arbor was Designed to help keep the Rock House Cool during the Heat of Summer. So, when the Grapes were Gone, the House got too Hot for him, which Caused him to Sell it to another Capitalist, who Decided that it Needed some Modifications, whereby it was further Permanently Damaged: beCause, his Modifications were Trespassing on Architectural Necessities, for which I Warned him; but, he Ignored it. †§‡§§

04-09 [_] So, O Selected King, he Weakened the Concrete Walls, which were Holding Up the Heavy 600-Ton Concrete Roof, which Needed Good Strong Secure Walls to Rest on, which Kept the House Alive, you might say, or in Good Working Condition; but, without those Strong Walls, it became like a Man with 2 Broken Legs when an Earthquake Struck, which was to be Expected: beCause, there had already been hundreds of Earthquakes in Brokelahoma: beCause of Fracking the Earth for Oil and Gas. Therefore, if the Rock House had not been Built on Solid Bedrock, it would have probably Collapsed; but, being Unnecessarily Weakened by an Ignorant Fool, it only Cracked the Ceiling, just to Remind him that there are Architectural RULES to Follow. Therefore, the Crack in the Ceiling is enough to SPOOK AWAY any Potential Buyers, who are Afraid that the entire Roof might Fall on them when they are Sleeping in the House, which is now Worthless!

04-10 [_] Well, my Friend, no one would Believe that a little Crack could make a Million-dollar House Worthless; but, I suppose that it could also make a Billion-dollar House Worthless, as in the Case of the Washington Cathedral, which Suffered with an Earthquake, which had to be Repaired at a Cost of Millions of Dollars. However, a Well-built Swanky Stone Dome Home Complex would not Suffer any Major Damages in Earthquakes: beCause of being Stabilized by very THICK Solid Walls, a Concrete Dome on every Room, and 10 to 40 feet of Dirt, Rocks, Sand, Gravel, and Clay on Top of those Domes, which are Covered with 3 to 4 Feet of Topsoil, which is Planted with Trees, Vines, and Gardens, which Ties it all Neatly Together. The Terrace Wall might look something like this, except that each Wall would be Miles Long, and at a 45° Angle! The Arcades of Wind Funnels would be at the Top of each Wall, instead of Houses, which would be Inside, behind the Thick Secure Stone Walls. The First Great Terrace would not even have Houses in it: beCause it should be and would be Up Above the Flood Plain by at least 100 Feet, or more. The Good News is the Fact that God Provided hundreds of thousands of Mountains of Rocks for us to Work with, if we are not too Lazy or Crazy to Do that. Even the Poor Rich Indians did it. †§‡

— Chapter 05 —

Be Aware of Snakes!

05-01 [_] When you Receive an E-mail that reads like this:

> You **cannot** get COVID-19 from the
> investigational vaccine or the placebo used
> as part of the study. The investigational
> vaccine will not increase your risk of
> COVID-19.

Be Aware of Snakes: beCause, the Truth could be just the Opposite. After all, Citizens have been Used and Abused by the Federal Government, many Times; but, in the Case of the Bug-19, they could use the "Placebo" to get Rid of Social Insecurity Recipients, whereby they could Save Billions of Dollars, by getting Rid of Old People, and especially of Black People and Brown People, who are "a threat to our national security." I am not saying that it is a Lie; but, that it could be a Lie: beCause, the American Indians, for Example, Heard lots of Promises that were not Kept.

05-02 [_] O Selected King, how do we Know for Sure that YOU are not Working for the Fake Government, which uses Orwellian Tactics — such as your Questionable Orwellian Symbols? †§

05-03 [_] Well, my Friend, I am perhaps the only Person that you can Trust about anything: beCause, all of my Lies and Deceptions are Harmless, while their Lies and Deceptions are for the Intent to Kill and Gain Wealth for some Rich Hogs, which they have Done many Times, as in the Case of Vietnam, which was about Keeping the Drug Trafficking in Burma going on, which was Reported in *"The Plain Truth"* Magazine, many Years Ago, which did an Extensive Investigation on it, which the Mainstream News Media stayed away from: beCause, they always take the Side of Uncle Sam, as does *Wikipedia,* which has been Caught Lying more than once, which Denies Legitimate Conspiracy Theories — such as the Evil Events of September 11th, 2001, which is easily Debunked by this one Incriminating Photograph on the next Page, which the Federal Burden of False Investigators (FBI) and the Central Unintelligent Agencies (CIA) have yet to Explain: beCause, there is only ONE Rational Explanation for it, which is Explained in: "Conspiracy Theories did it!" (The Evil Events of September 11th 2001 are Revisited by a Wise Son of King Solomon!) **By** The Worldwide People's Revolution!® Book 128. Therefore, no matter how many Lies the Propagandists Tell, you can be Sure that the Truth will eventually "Leak Out."

05-04 [_] O Selected King, I would have never Guessed that the War in Vietnam was all about Keeping the Drug Trafficking Operating; but, now that I have Studied the Situation in Afghanistan, which is all about Keeping the Poppy Plants Growing, it does make Good Sense: beCause, we are talking about Billions of Dollars in the Heroin and Morphine Industries. In Fact, the so-called "Wicked" Taliban had almost Wiped Out the Poppy Plants, when the American Troops arrived in Afghanistan, just in Time to Rescue them! And now, the Production has Increased by 27,000%! ‡

How does morphine work?

Morphine is from a group of medicines called opiates, or narcotics.

It works in the central nervous system and the brain to block pain signals to the rest of the body. It also reduces the anxiety and stress caused by pain.

When morphine blocks the pain, there are other unwanted effects, for example, slow or shallow breathing. It also slows down digestion, which is why morphine can cause constipation.

05-05 [_] WHO Sliced Off that Hardened Steel Column at the World Trade Center (WTC) Towers during September 11th, 2001? Airplanes cannot Do Sneaky Things like that, nor can Hijackers with Box Cutters. So, WHO did it? Answer: a Professional Demolition Team. Moreover, at that Time, there were only 6 such Capable Demolition Teams in the Whole World, and all of them were Israelis, or Working for Israelis. Therefore, it is no Surprise that CONgress would not Want their Pet Nation to be Exposed for what it is: beCause, that might Cause People to Think that maybe the Iranians and Palestinians have a Legitimate Cause of Mistrusting the Israeli Government and the American Federal Government, which is Notorious for Sneaky Acts of Kindness and Murder, for which Howard Zinn wrote a Documentary Book, called: **"A People's History of the United States,"** which Lists more than 500 All-American Atrocities! But, Poor Howard Died before getting around to Investigating the September 11th, 2001, False Flag Operation, which has been Thoroughly Investigated by the Architects and Engineers at: www.AE911Truth.org who made up a Famous YouTube Video, called: **Experts Speak Out,** which anyone can Watch on their Computer Screens, which brings up a hundred or more Unanswered Questions, which should be Answered at: "The GREAT Worldwide TELEVISED Court HEARING!" (That Great Meeting of the Most-Intelligent and Well-Educated Minds!) **By** The Worldwide People's Revolution!® Book 041B: beCause, the Real Criminals are still Walking Free, when they should be Behind Steel Bars in Maximum Security Prisons. For Example, Larry Silverstein gained about 6 Billion Dollars by the Evil Events of September 11th, 2001, while Little Dick Chicanery gained about 58 Billion Dollars, and George Warmonger Bush also gained a lot of Money; but, I am not Sure just how much. He should Know the Truth of it; and Osama bin Obama should Know just WHY he had Laden Murdered in Pakistan, when he used to be Working for the Trusted CIA. †§‡

05-06 [_] O Selected King, if you ever get yourself Entangled in that Spider Web of American Confusion, you will most likely also get yourself Assassinated: beCause, Murderers do not take Kindly to any Truths that might Expose them: beCause, they are like those Ancient Scribes and Pharisees, who Orchestrated the Murder of the Most-Righteous Man who ever Lived, and Blamed it onto the Romans, who were their Patsies. Nevertheless, we all Know for a Fact that it was brought about by those Lying Conniving Edomites, who have Ties with the Edomite Bankers, who Manage the Money Games, who Control the Money Supplies, who Determine WHO gets Rich, and who stays Poor: beCause, Money is POWER, which can get Things Done, which was Proven by Adolf Hitler, who Bucked Up Against those Edomites, who Played Games on both Sides of the War Game, just to Gain BILLIONS of Dollars by it: beCause, the Edomites are the Chief Weapons Manufacturers, who Love those Hateful Wars: beCause, they are Exempt from them, having far too many Bone Spurs, you might say. Therefore, for your own Safety, I Strongly Suggest that you Steer Clear of the Edomites, and leave that Larry Silverstein and his Distant Cousins alone: beCause, they have Ties with the Mafia and other Outlaws, whose Works are Done in the Dark.§‡

05-07 [_] Well, my Friend, it is Difficult to say what an Entangled Spider Web it is; but, I am no Great Threat to their Evil Empire, as of this Date: beCause, I am not very Popular; but, if my Inspired Books should Suddenly begin to Sell Well, I would Naturally be in Graveyard Danger! ‡

05-08 [_] ♦♦ O Selected King, if Osama bin Laden was Guilty of any Crimes, he should have been Arrested and brought to a Fair Trial, instead of being Murdered by American Thugs without Living Consciences, who should have Known that it is WRong to Assassinate anyone, no matter what they are Falsely Accused of: beCause, Murder is MURDER, no matter how you go about doing it. Justice Demands that the Accused Person must be Confronted Face-to-Face by his Accuser. †§‡§§

05-09 [_] Well, my Friend, I must Agree with you about that; but, most Americans do not seem to Agree with you, who put "National Interests" Ahead of "True Justice," who have Deep Concerns for the Financial Welfare of Rich Hogs on Wall Street, who do not Object to Lying nor Murdering Innocent Souls — such as the 30,000 or more Victims of the False Flag Operations during the September 11th, 2001, Capitalist VICTORY, which put about 6 Trillion Dollars into the Coffers of the Edomites! Yes, it is all Carefully Explained in Various Books, for whomever makes a Thorough Investigation into the Truth of it. After all, there is no Way that such Evils can be Hidden among the Walking Bushes; but, in Order to get some True Justice, we Desperately Need to Conduct: "The GREAT Worldwide TELEVISED Court HEARING!" Book 041B, whereby the Witnesses can Testify without any Fears: beCause of being Protected by "The New RIGHTEOUS One-World Government!" Book 056, which has nothing to Hide, nor is it

Concerned, Ashamed, Embarrassed, nor Intimidated by the Fact that Criminals should be Found Guilty as Charged, and Sentenced to Prisons: beCause, it is not Biased in any Way. Indeed, if the Iranians are Guilty as Charged, they should be Punished, which is also True for the Israelis.†§‡§§

05-10 [_] O Selected King, we all Know for a Fact that the Aggressors are the Israelis, who Forcefully took the Land of Palestine from the Poor Palestinians, even as the Europeans took the Land from the American Indians: beCause, at that Time it was Legal for the Aggressors to Conquer whomever they could Conquer: beCause, it did not Bother the Conscience of King David to Kill the Philistines: beCause, Jehovah God had COMMANDED him to Do so. However, God did NOT Command anyone to Murder the Indians, nor the Palestinians: beCause, God had nothing Against them, nor were they any Great Threat to his Good Government in Rome, which is at the Heart of all of these Issues: beCause, it is like that Spider's Web, which has Entangled many Nations in "Christian" Affairs, including Islamic Nations, which are also Guilty of Telling Lies, who Idolize Muhammad as a Prophet, who never gave so much as ONE True Prophecy; but, they call him the Holy Prophet, as if he were a Prophet, when he was only an Impostor and Religious Fanatic, who should be brought to COURT for his own Multitude of Humanitarian Crimes, who even Permitted his Soldiers to Sodomize their Enemies after the Battles were over, even as Saint Joseph Stalin Permitted his Soldiers to Rape 60,000 or more Women in Berlin, after World War 2 was Over: beCause, he was a Low-life Edomite Son of SATAN, who is still Praised by Deceived Russians! †§‡§§

— Chapter 06 —

Can anyone be Trusted?

06-01 [_] Was there ever a Time when anyone could be Trusted? Well, of course there was. For Example, I Trusted my Grandfather, who was always Honest, who had no Cause to Lie, nor did he Like any Lies. Moreover, if my Dad told someone that he would Do something, he Did it: beCause, his Word was as Good as Gold. I never Heard my Mother ever Tell a Lie. Therefore, I had no Reason for not Trusting her. The same was True for her 6 Brothers and 7 Sisters. None of them ever Lied to me. So, why should I not Trust them? President Richard (Tricky Dick) Nixon was the First Major Liar in my Life, who said: "I am not a Crook." But, he was a Crook: beCause, it is almost Impossible to become a Politician, without becoming a Liar. Indeed, even Mark Twain recognized the Fact, during the 1800s, that Writing Novels Required a certain amount of Lies, just to make the Stories Sound Good or Exciting enough for People to reed them. Indeed, the entire Novel is generally just one Big LIE, even if it is Based on Real-life Incidents. However, the *Holy Bible* is written as if there were no Lies in it, in spite of being Full of Lies and Deceptions: beCause, it is supposedly Historical, which starts right out telling about some Fake Creation, whereby the Stars were Created after the Earth was Created, as a Kind of After-Thot — "Oh, by the Way, God Created the Stars, also." Moreover, according to that Creation Story, God Created the Sunstar after he Created the Earth, when it is most likely that the Earth was Born from the Sunstar, and the Moon was Born from the Earth: beCause, the Earth is Hollow, by the same Size as the Moon, which is also Inhabited by tens of Billions of People, including those who like to Fly around in Flying Saucers and Big Cigar-shaped Spaceships, who come from other Worlds to Vacation here! †§‡ {See: "The Secret City of the Great King!" (HOW the True Church will Escape from the Great Tribulation!) By The Worldwide People's Revolution!® Book 042. Do not Doubt.}

1   06-02 [_] O Selected King of **The Worldwide People's Revolution,** can that be Proven — that
2   the Moon was Born from the Earth, and, that the Earth is Hollow, and Inhabited with Giants on
3   the Inside of it? Is *Psalm 48* Actually True — that Mount Zion is on the Inside of the Earth? †§‡§§
4

5
6
7   06-03 [_] Well, my Friend, if I were a Liar, I could tell you that the above Picture was taken on
8   the Inside of the Earth, and you would Naturally Believe me, if you were Naïve, like many Silly
9   Americans, who Sincerely Believe that Osama bin Laden Orchestrated all of the Evil Events of
10   September 11th, 2001, from his Cave Hideout in Afghanistan, whose Airplane Hijackers Sliced
11   Off that Hardened Steel Column with their Box Cutters, just after Delivering the Passport of the
12   Chief Hijacker in Pristine Condition to a Sidewalk in New York City, which was the First Sign of
13   a Conspiracy Theory in Action: beCause, HOW could a Thing like that Happen? The Passport
14   would have been in the Pocket or Briefcase of the Hijacker. Therefore, HOW would it go about
15   Landing itself in Pristine Condition on the Sidewalk? Why did it not bring the Body with it, or at
16   least the Briefcase? How did it get Out of the Airplane? Awe, "the Airplane EXPLODED UPON
17   IMPACT," you say. Was that Before the Airplane went through the Tower, or after it Retracted
18   itself from the other Side of the Tower, seeing that there is a Video Picture of that Retraction?
19   Maybe the Passport got Out of the Briefcase by the Help of some Holy Angel, who was Working
20   for the Central Unintelligent Agencies? In Fact, maybe it was all Faked by the Federal Burden of
21   False Investigations, which never even Discovered that Sliced Off Hardened Steel Column, which
22   was not Mentioned in 600+ pages of *The 911 Commission Report,* among many other Fascinating
23   Details — such as the WRong 747 6-Ton Titanium Jet Engine that was Conveniently Discovered
24   on the Lawn at the Pentagon, the Day AFTER it Crashed into the Pentagon, and BOUNCED OFF
25   of the Unbroken Window, and Placed itself about 100 feet Short of its Target, while Traveling at
26   about 600 Miles per Hour (MpH), rather than Follow the Natural Law of Isaac Newton's Inertia!‡

Law of inertia, also called Newton's first law, postulate in physics that, if a body is at rest or moving at a constant speed in a straight line, it will remain at rest or keep moving in a straight line at constant speed unless it is acted upon by a force.

www.britannica.com › Science › Physics

law of inertia | Discovery, Facts, & History | Britannica

06-04 [_] ♦♦♦♦♦♦♦ Believe it or not, there was no Magic Force that Grabbed those 2 6-Ton Titanium Jet Engines by their Ball Bearings, and Flung them AWAY from the Hardened Concrete Wall of the Pentagon, while they were Traveling at 600+ MpH! What Force could that have been? Tell us where that Force would have come from? Believe it or not, we are Able (though not everyone is Willing) to Duplicate the Scene of the Crime, by Remotely Guiding another Airplane into the Pentagon (loaded down with 200-pound Hogs, Fastened Securely with their Seat Belts), or into some similar Wall, just to Discover whether or not we might Duplicate such a Reaction to the Action of getting one of those Hogs to Pilot that Experimental Airplane. I would Bet everything in Heaven and on Earth that no such Things could Happen during a Million Experiments, including the Landing of a Pristine Passport on a Sidewalk in New Yuck City, from an Airplane that EXPLODES Inside of a Concrete and Steel Tower that also Slices Off a half-dozen Steel Columns every 32 feet, just to make them Convenient to Load onto Transport Trucks, to be Hauled away to a Shipyard, and Delivered to a Steel Mill in China, for Free, to be Recycled for Building Steel Bridges between the Minds of Reason and Logic, with Osama bin Laden Holding Up both Ends of 50,000 or more American Lies! (Yes, Sweetheart, it is called a "Metaphor" by Word Craftsmen, who could have done a much Better Construction Job on *The 911 Commission Report,* if they had simply Discovered a Key Word in their Dictionary, called: HONESTY.) The Truth was never brought into any Courtroom for Questioning about any of the Evil Events of September 11ᵗʰ, 2001. †§‡§§

06-05 [_] ♦♦♦ O Selected King, are you saying that several Murder Crimes were Committed during September 11ᵗʰ, 2001, and not even ONE Trial was Conducted by the Low Court of Supreme Injustices, who should have been the First Intelligent People to SEE that those 24 Hardened Steel Columns in 3 WTC Towers did not just Slice Off themselves every 32 feet, whereby they might be Conveniently Loaded onto Transport Trucks, and Hauled away to China, India, or wherever? Indeed, among the 67,564 Lawyers and Judges in New York City, not ONE of them even Demanded a TRIAL, where the Evidences at the Scene of the Crime might be Presented with the Testimonies of Eyewitnesses and Earwitnesses: beCause it was just PRESUMED that Osama bin Laden and his Gang of Thugs carried it all out from the Advantage Point of a Cave in Afghanistan! †§‡§§

How many lawyers are in the U.S.? The total number of lawyers in the United States has seen little increase in the last few years; in 2020, there were **1.33 million lawyers** in the U.S. – virtually unchanged from the previous year, and not much above the 2015 figure of **1.3 million**. Nov 4, 2020

www.statista.com › Services › Business Services

• U.S.: number of lawyers 2007-2020 | Statista

As of 2017, **there** are around 1.3 million licensed and practicing **attorneys in the United States**, which roughly translates to one **lawyer** for every 244 Americans. ... This is why the market has **too many lawyers**: because **there** are not enough people who will need legal services. Nov 23, 2018

www.thecareercookbook.com › too-many-lawyers

Avoid Law School, The Job Market Has Too Many Lawyers | The ...

06-06 [_] ♦♦♦♦ Well, not only that, my Friend, among all of those Lawyers, not one of them was Allowed near to those Crime Scenes during nor after September 11th, 2001: beCause, there were no Criminal Investigations until 5 Years LATER: beCause, President George Warmonger Bush and Little Dick Chicanery had everything Under their Control; but, please do not Ask me HOW: beCause, I have no Idea how thousands of People could be Murdered, and not one Lawyer was Interested in a TRIAL of any Kind? Yes, I find that most Amazing; but, what is even more Amazing is the Fact that not until this very Day are Americans Crying Out for JUSTICE for Osama bin Laden, who was the PATSY, who was Blamed for Slicing Off those Hardened Steel Columns, which none of those Lawyers, nor any of their Undercover Secret Investigators Discovered: beCause, they all just PRESUMED that Osama bin Laden did it with the Help of his 19 Hijackers from Saudi Arabia and from the Sphinx Territory in Egypt, which is Famous for Slight-of-Hand Operations in Biblical Proportions! For Example, Egyptian Historians all Agree that Ramses II Lived for 90 Years, and did NOT Drown in the Red Sea, as the Biblical Fairy Tale tells it. †§‡§§

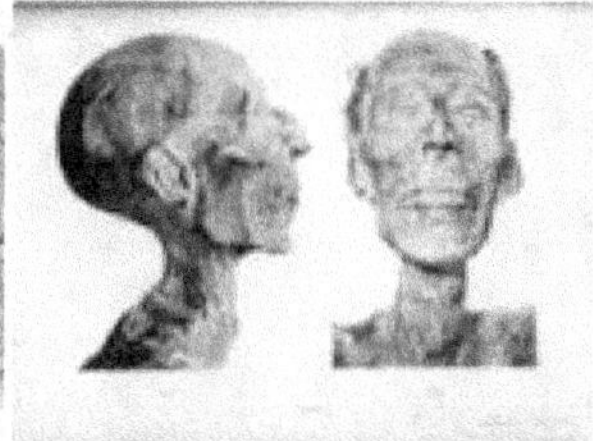

Estimates of his **age** at **death** vary; 90 or 91 is considered most likely. **Ramesses II** celebrated an unprecedented thirteen or fourteen Sed festivals (the first held after 30 years of a pharaoh's reign, and then, every three years) during his reign—more than any other pharaoh.

Place of death: Pi-Ramesses

Place of burial: Valley of the Kings, KV7, The E...

en.wikipedia.org › wiki › Ramesses_II

Ramesses II - Wikipedia

{**FOOTNOTE 01:** There is an Uncanny Resemblance between the Appearance of Ramses II and Anwar Sadat. Perhaps he was the Reincarnation of Ramses II? But, A-[_] I Doubt it. B-[_] God Knows. C-[_] Nobody Knows. D-[_] There is no such a Thing as Reincarnation.}

Anwar Sadat

محمد أنور السادات

Anwar Sadat in 1980

3rd President of Egypt

Ramses II (r. 1279-1213 BC) was undoubtedly the greatest pharaoh of the 19th Dynasty – and one of the most important leaders of ancient Egypt. The ostentatious pharaoh is best remembered for his exploits at the Battle of Kadesh, his architectural legacy, and for bringing Egypt into its golden age. Feb 3, 2020

www.historyhit.com › facts-about-ramses-ii

10 Facts About Ramses II – History Hit

The identity of Pharaoh in the Moses story has been much debated, but many scholars are inclined to accept that Exodus has King **Ramses II** in mind. ... These two cities are quite possibly the **biblical Ramses** and Pithom. Dec 28, 2018

www.nationalgeographic.com › people-in-the-bible › pha...

Who was the Egyptian pharaoh challenged Moses?

{**FOOTNOTE 02:** The Person should have Asked, What Egyptian Pharaoh challenged Moses, according to Egyptian History? Answer: NONE. Not even the *Holy Bible* makes it Clear.}

Was Ramses II a good leader?

The pharaoh **Ramses II** (RAM-seez) ruled from about 1290 to 1224 B.C.E., during the New Kingdom. Called **Ramses** the **Great**, he is one of the most famous pharaohs. He reigned for more than 60 years, longer than almost any other pharaoh. He is best known for his military **leadership** and for building numerous monuments.

sites.google.com › site › 8---the-ancient-egyptian-pharaohs

8.6 - Pharaoh Ramses II: Military Leader and Master Builder -

When did Moses lead the Israelites out of Egypt?

1300

1300 BCE - the beginning of a religion

Moses led the Jews out of slavery in **Egypt** and **led** them to the Holy Land that God had promised them. The escape of the **Jews** from **Egypt** is remembered by **Jews** every year in the festival of Passover. Jul 6, 2009

www.bbc.co.uk › religions › judaism › history › moses_1

Religions - Judaism: Moses - BBC

How long were the Israelites in Egypt?

430 years

The Book of Exodus itself attempts to ground the event firmly in history, dating the exodus to the 2666th year after creation (Exodus 12:40-41), the construction of the tabernacle to year 2667 (Exodus 40:1-2, 17), stating that the Israelites dwelled in Egypt for **430 years** (Exodus 12:40-41), and including place names ...

en.wikipedia.org › wiki › The_Exodus

The Exodus - Wikipedia

{**FOOTNOTE 03:** The Scholars cannot Agree on any Exact Dates: beCause the Bible is not a Reliable History Book, which does not even Name the Pharaoh at the Time of the Exodus!}

What was Ramses II greatest achievement?

Perhaps the best-known **achievements** of **Ramesses II** are his architectural endeavors, building more monuments than any other pharaoh, most notably the Ramesseum and the temples of Abu Simbel south in Aswan. Sep 12, 2019

www.osiristours.com › great-king-ramesses-ii

Who Was The Great King Ramesses II? - Osiris Tours

1

What made Ramses II Great?

Military Leader

During his reign as pharaoh, **Ramses II led** the Egyptian army against several enemies including the Hittites, Syrians, Libyans, and Nubians. He expanded the Egyptian empire and secured its borders against attackers. Perhaps the most famous battle during **Ramses**' rule was the Battle of Kadesh.

www.ducksters.com › history › ancient_egypt › ramses_ii

Ancient Egyptian Biography for Kids: Ramses II - Ducksters

2

Which Pharaoh drowned in the Red Sea?

Pharaoh, Haman

The **Pharaoh**, Haman, and their army in chariots pursuing the fleeing children of Israel **drowned in the Red Sea** as the parted water closed up on them. The **Pharaoh's** submission to God at the moment of death and total destruction was rejected but his dead body was saved as a lesson for posterity and he was mummified.

en.wikipedia.org › wiki › Haman_(Islam)

Haman (Islam) - Wikipedia

3
4
5 {**FOOTNOTE 04:** Please Notice that the Muslims have their own Versions of what Happened at
6   the Red Sea. No Egyptian History mentions the 7 Years of Biblical Famine in Exodus.}

Is Joseph found in Egyptian history?

The idea of a foreigner reaching the top of **Egyptian** society sounds unlikely and there is no archaeological or written record of a Prime Minister in **Egypt** called **Joseph**. However some new scientific evidence helps to support the case of a **historical Joseph**. Jul 6, 2009

www.bbc.co.uk › religion › religions › judaism › history

Religions - Judaism: Joseph - BBC

7

What caused the famine in Egypt?

Summary: An environmental drama played out on the world stage in the late 18th century when a volcano killed 9,000 Icelanders and brought a **famine** to **Egypt** that reduced the population of the Nile valley by a sixth. Nov 22, 2006

www.sciencedaily.com › releases › 2006/11

Icelandic Volcano Caused Historic Famine In Egypt, Study Shows

The investigators used a computer model developed by NASA's Goddard Institute for Space Studies to trace atmospheric changes that followed the 1783 eruption of Laki in southern Iceland back to their point of origin. The study is the first to conclusively establish the linkage between high-latitude eruptions and the water supply in North Africa.

Summary: An environmental drama played out on the world stage in the late 18th century when a volcano killed 9,000 Icelanders and brought a famine to Egypt that reduced the population of the Nile valley by a sixth. A study by three scientists demonstrates a connection between these two widely separated events, and is the first to conclusively establish the linkage between high-latitude eruptions and the water supply in North Africa.

{**FOOTNOTE 05:** That is no Proof that any such Volcano took place in Iceland around 1300 B.C., nor that Egypt Suffered a Great Famine at that Time. Just the Fact that Egyptian History does not Mention that Great Famine, Joseph, Jacob, nor Israelite Slaves is Dumbfounding! It would be like American History Books not Mentioning the Revolutionary War, Civil War, nor the Evil Events of September 11th, 2001. Indeed, if the Biblical Account of the Famine is True, it was a Major Event: beCause, "ALL Nations" were Affected by it. People came to Egypt from ALL Nations, if you can Believe it, just to Survive! However, it is not Confirmed by any other Histories of other Nations! Notice that the Ignorant People, who Ask Google their Questions, have no Idea how to Properly Construct their Questions. "Who was the Pharaoh during the Time of Moses in the Bible?" is more Accurate. BUT, there was no such Person called "Moses."}

Who was the Pharaoh during Moses?

Ramses II

If this is true, then the oppressive pharaoh noted in Exodus (1:2–2:23) was **Seti I** (reigned 1318–04), and the pharaoh during the Exodus was **Ramses II** (c. 1304–c. 1237). In short, Moses was probably born in the late 14th century bce. Jan 10, 2020

www.britannica.com › biography › Moses-Hebrew-prophet

Moses | Story, Summary, Significance, & Facts | Britannica

What was found in Ramses II tomb?

His funerary temple, the Ramesseum, **contained** a massive library of some 10,000 papyrus scrolls. He honored both his father and himself by completing temples at Abydos. For all of **Ramses II's** efforts to ensure his legacy would live on, there was one testament to his power he could not have foreseen. May 13, 2019

www.nationalgeographic.com › people › reference › rams...

Ramses II—facts and information - National Geographic

06-07 [_] Interestingly enough, not one of those Scrolls Mentioned Moses, Jacob, Joseph, nor any Israelites, at all: beCause, they were no Part of Egyptian History. Moreover, the *Holy Bible* does not Mention the Pyramids, nor any of the Egyptian Monuments; but, only "Treasure Cities" made of MUD Bricks, which have Conveniently Disappeared! (Please Check the Boxes with Statements that you Agree with. Remember that it was no easy Thing to Edit a Scroll, which had to be Totally Re-written. Therefore, if the Egyptians were Attempting to Edit OUT any Mention of Moses, or of the Children of Israel, they would have no doubt been Forced to Edit at least 9,000 Scrolls!)

Did Ramses II build a pyramid?

In the third year of his reign, **Ramesses** started the most ambitious **building** project after the **pyramids**, which were built almost 1,500 years earlier. ... **Ramesses II** erected more colossal statues of himself than any other pharaoh, and also usurped many existing statues by inscribing his own cartouche on them.

en.wikipedia.org › wiki › Ramesses_II

Ramesses II - Wikipedia

His **body** was originally entombed in the Valley of the Kings, as was customary for a pharaoh, but ancient Egyptian priests later moved it to thwart rampant looters. In 1881, **Ramesses II's** mummy was **discovered** in a secret royal cache at Deir el-Bahri, along with those of more than 50 other rulers and nobles. May 28, 2013

www.history.com › news › 5-great-mummy-discoveries

5 Great Mummy Discoveries - HISTORY

{**FOOTNOTE 06:** It is Interesting that no one during Ancient Times could figure out HOW to Stop the Looters. They Tried Burying the Tombs under Sand, and it sometimes Worked; but, being Stone Workers, why not Bury each Tomb of a King under a HUGE Stone, which would have Required thousands of Men to Move such Stones, which would have Deterred the Looters, who would not have been Happy with getting a Small Percentage of the Loot. In Fact, the Egyptian Government could have gotten very Bold, and Inscribed a Complete History of each King on the Inside of the Tomb, which could have a 1,000-Ton Rock Resting on Top of the Tomb, being Designed to Fall on whomever Disturbed it too much. We have the Lincoln Memorial for a Good Example of how to Construct a Proper Tomb for Kings. Do you know that there are 200 Tons of Gold Bricks buried under Lincoln's Statue? No, you never knew it! †§‡§§}

Which Ramses fought Moses?

Pharaoh Ramses II

Ramses II became king as a teenager and reigned for 67 years. He aspired to defeat the Hittites and control all of Syria, but in the fifth year of his reign Ramses walked into a Hittite trap laid for him at Kadesh, on the Orontes River in Syria.

www.britannica.com › biography › Moses-Hebrew-prophet

Moses - Moses and Pharaoh | Britannica

Why did SETI kill the babies?

The Pharaoh had decreed that all their **baby** boys **were** to be thrown into the Nile, because he feared that they might become too powerful. When Moses, her youngest **child**, was born, Jochebed hid him for three months until she could hide him no longer.

en.wikipedia.org › wiki › Jochebed

Jochebed - Wikipedia

06-08 [_] Please Notice that Wickedpedia gets its Information from the *Holy Bible,* while I get my Information from the Reliable Trustworthy Egyptian Historians, who Actually have Monuments and Dead Bodies to Prove that such People Lived. To the Contrary, not ONE Body nor Tomb of any Ancient Biblical Character has been Discovered! The Tombs of Abraham, Isaac, Jacob and Joseph, for Example, are supposed to be in a Cave at Machpelah, according to *Genesis 23, and Related Scriptures,* which Cave and Remains have yet to be Discovered: beCause, the Account is as Fake as that Saudi Arabian Passport on the Sidewalk in New Yuck City. Indeed, even if the Tomb of Father Abraham was Stolen by the Hittites, what about the Tombs of Isaac, Jacob, and Joseph in the same Cave. Did the Resurrected Hittites also Steal their Tombs? Not likely. What about the Tomb of King David, which was supposedly still around at the Time of Saint Peter in *Acts 2:29,* which no one has Discovered? Was/were David and King Solomon for REAL? If so, where are their Tombs? Awe, "the Romans Destroyed them," you say. What for? Greeks and Romans Revered War Heroes. They always Honored the Dead Heroes, even of their Enemies: beCause they were like the Gods to them. In Fact, almost all of the Ancient War Heroes have Tombs to Prove it. But, Poor WISE Rich Boy, King Solomon, did not Manage to make a Proper Tomb for himself, which Saint Peter might Mention, nor was anyone Interested in Preserving any such Tombs for Adam, Melchizedek, Abraham, Isaac, Jacob Joseph, Moses, Joshua, Gideon, Samson, Samuel, nor anyone else of Biblical Fame! WHY? How come one of those Apostles never Mentioned the Cave of Machpelah? Had it already been Lost by the Time of Christ? Where is the Field by the Cave? It must have been a Special Field, just for Wealthy Abraham to Buy it. †§‡§§

06-09 [_] O Selected King, if the *Holy Bible* is nothing but Jewish MYTHS, or Jewish FABLES, as the Apostle Paul called them in *Titus 1:14,* WHO can we Trust? Why should we Trust anything that is written in the Unholy Mutilated Bible, which is Full of Lies, which is Proven in: "The Peabrain Peacock Studies Demon-ocracy!" (A Guaranteed Solution for the Plastic Trash Problem!) **By The Worldwide People's Revolution!® Book 141, which Lists Contradictions? ‡**

Some Egyptologists believe that immediately before Tutankhamun's reign in the fourteenth century bc, **Nefertiti**, whose daughter was married to Tutankhamun, briefly ruled as pharaoh. Her **tomb** in the Valley of the Kings has never been **found**.
Feb 19, 2020

Who was Pharaoh in the Ten Commandments?

Pharaoh Rameses I of Egypt

After hearing the prophecy of the deliverer, Pharaoh **Rameses I** of Egypt orders the death of all newborn Hebrew males. Yochabel saves her infant son by setting him adrift in a basket on the Nile.

en.wikipedia.org › wiki › The_Ten_Commandments_(19...

The Ten Commandments (1956 film) - Wikipedia

06-10 [_] If you really Want to Learn the Whole Truth about it all, you only have to Consult the Movie Makers — such as Cecil B. DeMille, who Based *The Ten Commandments* movie on Historical FACTS, which were Researched by Various Jewish Scholars, who Assisted him to get it Right with a Capital R, just like the FBI Assisted President George Warmonger Bush to get it Right concerning the Evil Events of September 11th, 2001, whereby he made his Attack on Iraq!

Hollywood, California, U.S. **Cecil** Blount **DeMille** (/ˈsɛsəl dəˈmɪl/; August 12, 1881 – January 21, 1959) was an American film director and producer. Between 1914 and 1958, he made 70 features, both silent and sound films. ... His films were distinguished by their epic scale and by his cinematic showmanship.

Film: The Ten Commandments, Samson and D...

Born: August 12, 1881, Ashfield, Massachusetts

Parents: Henry Churchill de Mille, Beatrice de...

en.wikipedia.org › wiki › Cecil_B._DeMille

Cecil B. DeMille - Wikipedia

Cecil Blount **DeMille** was a founder of the Hollywood motion-picture industry, one of the most commercially successful producer-directors of his time, and one of the most influential filmmakers in history. Between 1914 and 1956, he made seventy feature films; all but seven were profitable.

www.cecilbdemille.com › biography

Biography – Cecil B. DeMille

Is the movie The Ten Commandments biblically accurate?

In terms of **accuracy** about Moses and his time, The **Ten Commandments** is patchy, regardless of whether you believe the **Biblical** version or prefer sceptical history. Nonetheless, it is a fascinating historical **film** — not for what it says about Moses, but for what it says about the cold war. Dec 18, 2008

www.theguardian.com › film › dec › ten-commandments-...

The Ten Commandments: An interesting insight into the cold war |

What does covet mean in the Ten Commandments?

You shall not covet

"You shall not **covet**" **means** that we should banish our desires for whatever **does** not belong to us. Never having enough money is regarded as a symptom of the love of money. Obedience to the tenth **commandment** requires that envy be banished from the human heart.

en.wikipedia.org › wiki › Thou_shalt_not_covet

Thou shalt not covet - Wikipedia

06-11 [_] How could you "never have enough money," if you Lived in a Beautiful Swanky PALACE? What would you Need with any Money, at all? Awe, you might want to take a Ride in your Rolls-Royce Car to the next Swanky Palace, instead of taking the Subway Train; but, there are no Dangerous Highways within Swanky Fortresses. Besides that, you might Pass by a Royal Swanky Buffet, which you would Naturally have to OWN, before you could Eat there, if you were a True Capitalist. Indeed, Communists and Socialists could not even Enjoy their Meals at any such Buffets: beCause of not OWNING them! Poor Creatures. We should Weep for those Babies. †§‡§§

en.wikipedia.org › wiki › Cecil_B._DeMille

Cecil B. DeMille - Wikipedia

DeMille's mother Beatrice, a literary agent and scriptwriter, whose parents were both of German-Jewish heritage, married Henry deMille July 1, 1876, despite her ...

Died: January 21, 1959 (aged 77); Hollywood...   Years active: 1899–1958
Nationality: American   Born: Cecil Blount DeMille; August 12, 188...

The Ten Commandments · The King of Kings · The Squaw Man · Agnes de Mille

06-12 [_] Wikipedia Admits that the Exodus was a Founding MYTH of the Israelis. Who can Argue against that Provable Truth? No Hebrew Graves have ever been Discovered in Egypt. No Stations of the Exodus have ever been Discovered, which I have Proven in other Inspired Books; but, no one is Asked to Trust me: beCause, I only have the Internet Information to go by, which could be WRong, which is most likely Rong; but, if the Masses of People have no Interest in Proving it, one Way or the other Way, how will we ever Learn the Whole Truth about anything? Not even the Site of the Crucifixion has been Found. The Best Solution is to DEMAND: "The GREAT Worldwide TELEVISED Court HEARING!" (That Great Meeting of the Most-Intelligent and Well-Educated Minds!) **By The Worldwide People's Revolution!® B-041B. ‡**

FOOTNOTE 07: The Space below is Reserved for any Rebuttals against my last Statement. Please Notice that no one had any Rebuttals to Send to me. My E-mail Address is found on the Outside of the Back Cover, near to the Bottom of the Page. If you cannot Find it, please Ask someone for some Help. Most People in this World of Wonders are Extra Happy to Help whomever Asks; and I am now Asking you to Ask them for Help, even if you do not Need it. †§‡§§

— Chapter 07 —

WHY Americans Want
a Righteous King to Govern them!

07-01 [_] "O King David, please Return," you say — please have Mercy on us Americans, and Deliver us from the Trumpites, Edomites, Canaanites, Hittites, Hivites, Hypocritters, Liars, and Mythmakers. Yes, we Desperately Need **"The New RIGHTEOUS One-World Government,"** seeing that China is about to Exploit a Trillion Gallons of Crude Oil in Ethiopia, which will Counteract all of the Green Energy Efforts that Dr. Biden and his Climate-Change Warriors will be Able to Obtain by Building Swanky Fortresses with Arcades of Stone Funnels for Wind Generators. In other Words, if the Chinese Produce 20 Gas-powered Electric Power Plants, next Year, they will Raise the Climate Change Performance Index by 10 Times more than we will Reduce that Index with Zero Emissions of Carbon Dioxide by the Year 2060, or even 2090. †§‡§§

07-02 [_] Well, my Friend, I am not Sure that the Normal American Understands what you Mean by the "Climate Change Performance Index," but, I am Sure that it Means something to you.

www.climate-change-performance-index.org

Climate Change Performance Index

The Climate Change Performance Index (CCPI) evaluates and compares the climate protection performance of more than 58 countries. The CCPI is an ...

Country Results · Downloads · Methodology · About

What is climate change index?

The MSCI Climate Change Indexes consider both the opportunities and risks associated with transition to a low carbon economy, enabling institutional investors and wealth managers to integrate climate risk considerations in their global equity investment process.

www.msci.com › ... › MSCI Climate Indexes

MSCI Climate Change Indexes - MSCI

Which country topped the Climate Change Performance Index?

In this year's index, **Sweden** leads the ranking on rank 4, followed by Denmark (5) and **Morocco** (6). The bottom five in this year's CCPI are Islamic Republic of **Iran** (57), Republic of Korea (58), **Chinese Taipei** (59), **Saudi Arabia** (60) and the United States (61), rated low or very low across almost all categories. Aug 8, 2020

www.manifestias.com › 2020/08/08 › climate-change-per...

Climate Change Performance Index -2020 - Manifest IAS

Who published climate change performance?

New **Climate** Institute, Germanwatch and the **Climate** Action Network (CAN) **released** the **2020 Climate Change Performance Index** (**CCPI**), which tracks the greenhouse gas (GHG) emissions of 57 countries and the EU.

empowerias.com › blog › prelims-special-facts › climate-c...

Climate Change Performance Index 2020 "EMPOWER IAS ...

1

What are the dangers of climate change?

More frequent and intense drought, storms, heat waves, rising sea levels, melting glaciers and **warming** oceans can directly harm animals, destroy the places they live, and wreak havoc on people's livelihoods and communities. As climate change worsens, dangerous weather events are becoming more frequent or severe.

www.worldwildlife.org › threats › effects-of-climate-change

Effects of Climate Change | Threats | WWF

2

What is the world doing to stop climate change?

But many of the **world's** major greenhouse gas emitters have already set national targets to **reduce** emissions, and they're forging their own initiatives to meet those goals. Some are focusing on curbing deforestation and boosting renewable energy sources. Dec 9, 2011

www.npr.org › 2011/12/07 › what-countries-are-doing-to...

What Countries Are Doing To Tackle Climate Change : NPR

3

Which country has the best climate policy?

Denmark

Denmark tops the list of **countries** doing the most to protect the environment, and continues to set ambitious goals, among them **having** at least half its energy consumption come from renewables by 2030 and to be independent of fossil fuels by 2050. Jul 14, 2019

www.usatoday.com › story › money › 2019/07/14 › clim...

Climate change: Countries doing most, least to protect environment

4
5
6   {Someone should Notify the Officials in Denmark that Swanky Fortresses can make it Possible
7   to have Zero Emissions within only 6 Years, and Total Independence from Fossil Fuels by 2030.
8   However, we would have to Employ **"Seven Great Armies of Working Soldiers!" (HOW to**
9   **Provide a Way for Everyone to WORK: so as to Eliminate Poverty, Crimes, Drug Abuses,**
10 **Prisons and Unnecessary Taxes!) By The Worldwide People's Revolution!® Book 015B.}**

Which countries are most affected by climate change?

The Arctic, Africa, small islands and Asian megadeltas are regions that are likely to be especially **affected** by future **climate change**. Africa is one of the **most vulnerable** continents to **climate** variability and **change** because of multiple existing stresses and low adaptive capacity.

en.wikipedia.org › wiki › Regional_effects_of_climate_ch...

Regional effects of climate change - Wikipedia

What country produces the most pollution?

China

The 20 countries that emitted the most carbon dioxide in 2018

Rank	Country	CO_2 emissions (total)
1	China	10.06GT
2	United States	5.41GT
3	India	2.65GT
4	Russian Federation	1.71GT

17 more rows

www.ucsusa.org › resources › each-countrys-share-co2-e...

Each Country's Share of CO2 Emissions | Union of Concerned ...

How much does the US contribute to climate change?

The **United States** produced 6.7 billion metric tons of carbon dioxide equivalent greenhouse gas (GHG) emissions in 2018, the second largest in the world after greenhouse gas emissions by China and among the worst countries by greenhouse gas emissions per person.

en.wikipedia.org › wiki › Greenhouse_gas_emissions_by...

Greenhouse gas emissions by the United States - Wikipedia

Published annually since 2005, the Climate Change Performance Index (**CCPI**) is an independent monitoring tool for tracking the climate protection performance of 57 countries and the EU.

germanwatch.org › CCPI

Climate Change Performance Index | Germanwatch e.V.

What is Denmark doing for climate change?   ∧

One country, however, has committed to making **climate** neutrality happen — and soon: **Denmark**'s parliament overwhelmingly passed an aggressive new **climate** law on Dec. ... The legislation aims to reduce the country's carbon emissions to 70% below its 1990 levels by 2030, with carbon neutrality targeted for 2050. Jan 7, 2020

www.usnews.com › news › best-countries › articles › den...

Denmark's Aggressive New Climate Law Blazes Path for Developed ...

What are some causes of climate change?   ∧

Humans are increasingly influencing the **climate** and the earth's temperature by burning fossil fuels, cutting down rainforests and farming livestock. This adds enormous amounts of greenhouse gases to those naturally occurring in the atmosphere, increasing the greenhouse effect and **global warming**.

ec.europa.eu › clima › change › causes_en

Causes of climate change | Climate Action - European Commission

What is climate crisis?   ∧

Climate crisis is a term describing global warming and **climate change**, and their consequences. The term has been used to describe the threat of global warming to the planet, and to urge aggressive **climate change** mitigation.

en.wikipedia.org › wiki › Climate_crisis

Climate crisis - Wikipedia

What are 5 effects of climate change?   ∧

Increased heat, drought and insect outbreaks, all linked to **climate change**, have increased wildfires. Declining water supplies, reduced agricultural yields, health **impacts** in cities due to heat, and flooding and erosion in coastal areas are additional concerns.

climate.nasa.gov › effects

The Effects of Climate Change - NASA Climate Change

Climate change is breeding storms with heavier rainfall, flooding farms — such as this **one**, which grows cotton. A warmer world — even by a half-degree Celsius — has more evaporation, leading to more water in the atmosphere. Such **changing** conditions put our agriculture, health, water supply and more at risk.

www.edf.org › climate › why-fighting-climate-change-so-...

This is why fighting climate change is so urgent | Environmental ...

> Even if we **stopped** emitting greenhouse gases today, **global warming** would continue
> to happen for at least several more decades, if not centuries. ... But it may not be **too**
> **late** to avoid or limit some of the worst effects of **climate change**.

climate.nasa.gov › faq › is-it-too-late-to-prevent-climate-c...

Is it too late to prevent climate change? – Climate Change: Vital ...

What is China doing to reduce emissions?

Lessening the **Emissions** from Fossil Fuels

China has made a concerted effort to **reduce** industrial **emissions**. In 2018, Beijing
introduced an action plan that requires 480 million tons of carbon capacity from steel
production to meet "ultra-low **emission**" standards by 2020.

chinapower.csis.org › china-greenhouse-gas-emissions

How is China Managing its Greenhouse Gas Emissions ...

Top 10 things you can do about climate change

1. Urge Ottawa to support a green recovery. ...
2. Use energy wisely — and save money too! ...
3. Get charged up with renewables. ...
4. Eat for a **climate**-stable planet. ...
5. Start a **climate** conversation. ...
6. Green your commute. ...
7. Consume less, waste less, enjoy life more. ...
8. Invest in renewables and divest from fossil fuels.

More items...

davidsuzuki.org › what-you-can-do › top-10-ways-can-st...

Top 10 things you can do about climate change - David Suzuki .

07-03 [_] Please Notice that none of those Top 10 Things mention anything about Constructing Swanky Fortresses, which is the one and ONLY Right Way to Solve the Climate Changing Problems: beCause of Solving 5,000+ other Problems, which we should have been Working on 40 Years Ago, when I first Proposed that Plan, in 1980. But, like now, I have not Managed to get any "Traction" or "Grip" on it: beCause, most People do not Like to Reed Books, and especially Books that Irritate them, which have more Truths than they can Tolerate, which bothers their Consciences.

07-04 [_] O Selected King, if you would give to me Permission, I could Edit your Uninspired Books, and make them more Readable and Sinner-friendly.

07-05 [_] Well, my Friend, certain Sincere People have already Tried Doing that, and were Defeated by it: beCause, my Inspired Books Address all Kinds of Important Subjects, which make them more Entertaining. Nevertheless, you are Welcome to Try it, if you Obtain my Written Permission, by Contacting my E-mail Address on the Back Cover. Chances are that you would be Defeated by the Multitude of Books to Deal with, as well as that Multitude of Important Subjects.

07-06 [_] O Selected King, the Reason that I am Longing for "The New RIGHTEOUS One-World Government," is to get Out of Paying Needless Taxes: beCause, that Good Government will simply Mint and Print the Necessary New Money — not to give it away, nor to Waste it on Needless Bankers; but, in Order to HIRE Working Soldiers to Build those "GLORIOUS Swanky Hotels Castles and Fortresses!" Book 019B, which will Represent that New Money, which will be the Best Money in all of this World of Wonders: beCause, it will have to be EARNED by Honest Labor, without any Loans, without any Insurance Scams, without Interest Robberies, and without any Hateful Taxes! Moreover, beCause of getting Paid GOOD Swanky Wages for any Extra "Overtime" Labor, we will have lots of Money to Donate to Missionary Work and Useful Organizations that Actually Help Poor People in Remote Places around the World. After all, we cannot Expect those Poor Ignorant Africans to be Building Swanky Fortresses in the Jungles! †§‡

07-07 [_] Well, my Friend, those Poor Ignorant Africans will be Happy to get the Assistance of their American-African Brothers, who will Naturally go over there to Help them, once they Discover how Nice those Swanky Fortresses are. In Fact, they will be Assisted by the United States Navy, Cargo Ships, and Cruise Ship Companies, just to get over there with the Right Equipment and Tools to Work with, who will Think of themselves as Compassionate Missionaries, who will bring Special Movies with them for those People to Watch, who will be Inspired to Help each other to Build those Glorious Fortresses in Africa, if they Want them. Indeed, it would be a Major Project, just to Build ONE such Fortress, in any one Country: beCause of the Horrible HEAT! But, they may take Ice Ships with them, just to Cool Off. After all, they will not be Limited by a Lack of Money, as People Used to be Limited under the Tyranny of Capitalism and Communism. †§‡§§

07-08 [_] O King David, I See that you have Revised your Way of Thinking during the Past 3,000 or so Years, whereby you no longer Want to Murder those Poor Africans, whom you used to Slaughter for the Fun of it, back in Biblical Times, when you Hated the Black People. So, I am now wondering what got into you? What Caused you to Change your Mind and Attitude toward them? Did Jesus Christ have something to Do with that, or what? Was he a Black Man, like you?‡

07-09 [_] Well, my Friend, King David is not here to Answer your Question; but, according to the *Holy Bible,* he will Arise and Govern all of Israel, according to *Jeremiah 30:9.*

Jer 30:9	But they shall serve the LORD their God, and David their king, whom I will raise up unto them.
Eze 34:23	And I will set up one shepherd over them, and he shall feed them, *even* my servant David; he shall feed them, and he shall be their shepherd.
Eze 34:24	And I the LORD will be their God, and my servant David a prince among them; I the LORD have spoken it.

Eze 37:22   And I will make them one nation in the land upon the mountains of Israel; and one king shall be king to them all: and they shall be no more two nations, neither shall they be divided into two kingdoms any more at all:

Eze 37:23   Neither shall they defile themselves any more with their idols, nor with their detestable things, nor with any of their transgressions: but I will save them out of all their dwellingplaces, wherein they have sinned, and will cleanse them: so shall they be my people, and I will be their God.

Eze 37:24   And David my servant *shall be* king over them; and they all shall have one shepherd: they shall also walk in my judgments, and observe my statutes, and do them.

Eze 37:25   And they shall dwell in the land that I have given unto Jacob my servant, wherein your fathers have dwelt; and they shall dwell therein, *even* they, and their children, and their children's children for ever: and my servant David *shall be* their prince for ever.

1

Amo 9:11   In that day will I raise up the tabernacle of David that is fallen, and close up the breaches thereof; and I will raise up his ruins, and I will build it as in the days of old:

2

Amo 9:12   That they may possess the remnant of Edom, and of all the heathen, which are called by my name, saith the LORD that doeth this.

Amo 9:13   Behold, the days come, saith the LORD, that the plowman shall overtake the reaper, and the treader of grapes him that soweth seed; and the mountains shall drop sweet wine, and all the hills shall melt.

Amo 9:14   And I will bring again the captivity of my people of Israel, and they shall build the waste cities, and inhabit *them*; and they shall plant vineyards, and drink the wine thereof; they shall also make gardens, and eat the fruit of them.

Amo 9:15   And I will plant them upon their land, and they shall no more be pulled up out of their land which I have given them, saith the LORD thy God.

3

| Act 15:16 | After this I will return, and will build again the tabernacle of David, which is fallen down; and I will build again the ruins thereof, and I will set it up: |

Act 15:16 — After this I will return, and will build again the tabernacle of David, which is fallen down; and I will build again the ruins thereof, and I will set it up:

Act 15:17 — That the residue of men might seek after the Lord, and all the Gentiles, upon whom my name is called, saith the Lord, who doeth all these things.

Act 15:18 — Known unto God are all his works from the beginning of the world.

Num 24:14 — "And now, indeed, I am going to my people. Come, I will advise you what this people will do to your people in the latter days."

Deu 4:30 — "When you are in distress, and all these things come upon you in the latter days, when you turn to the LORD your God and obey His voice

Isa 2:2 — Now it shall come to pass in the latter days
That the mountain of the LORD's house
Shall be established on the top of the mountains,
And shall be exalted above the hills;
And all nations shall flow to it.

Jer 30:24 — The fierce anger of the LORD will not return until He has done it,
And until He has performed the intents of His heart.

In the latter days you will consider it.

Eze 38:8 — "After many days you will be visited. In the latter years you will come into the land of those brought back from the sword *and* gathered from many people on the mountains of Israel, which had long been desolate; they were brought out of the nations, and now all of them dwell safely.

Eze 38:16 — "You will come up against My people Israel like a cloud, to cover the land. It will be in the latter days that I will bring you against My land, so that the nations may know Me, when I am hallowed in you, O Gog, before their eyes."

Dan 2:28   "But there is a God in heaven who reveals secrets,
and He has made known to King Nebuchadnezzar
what will be in the latter days. Your dream, and the
visions of your head upon your bed, were these:

Dan 10:14   "Now I have come to make you understand what will
happen to your people in the latter days, for the
vision *refers* to *many* days yet *to come."*

Mic 4:1   Now it shall come to pass in the latter days
That the mountain of the LORD's house
Shall be established on the top of the mountains,
And shall be exalted above the hills;
And peoples shall flow to it.

Rom 11:25   For I do not desire, brethren, that you should be
ignorant of this mystery, lest you should be wise in
your own opinion, that blindness in part has
happened to Israel until the fullness of the Gentiles
has come in.

07-10 [_] "There it is in a Nutshell," you might say; but, I will not go into the Details here: beCause, I have already Explained it all in other Good Books. *"Seek, and you shall Find,"* as Jesus sed. Why should I Bore you to Death with it? What Kind of a Kingdom did David have? Why was it so Great? Solomon was a Seer, who supposedly Visualized everything Past, Present and Future, who must have Known that I would be Born, and would Reveal what a Great Kingdom does for Money, since everything Revolves around MONEY! What can you Do without it? What can you Do with an Unlimited Amount of it? Try to Use your Great Imagination, O Leapfrog. What would you Do with an Unlimited Amount of Money? What would you Do, if you could get all Peoples to Love you and Obey you? Would you Command them to Build Wooden / Plastic Firetrap Trash Dumps, like Americans have done; or, would you get them to Build those **"GLORIOUS Swanky Hotels Castles and Fortresses!" (Beautiful Planned City States for WISE Intelligent Well-Educated People with Common Sense and Good Understanding!) By The Worldwide People's Revolution!®** Book 019B? Trust me, Climate Changes will Change your Mind, O Lady Doubtfulness. In Fact, you will be very "Lucky," if you get them Built before the Temperatures become Unbearable during the Daylight Hours. Remember that the Oceans can Rise by 21 feet, if all of the Ice should Melt, which would put much of the World Under the Water. Therefore, while there is still Fuel to Burn, it should be Used Wisely for Constructing Swanky Fortresses, and not be Wasted on Running Around in Endless Circles on Countless Highways of Confusion. Selah. ‡

— Chapter 08 —

Put Up your Best Arguments, O Environmentalists!

08-01 [_] O Selected King of **"The Worldwide People's Revolution,"** I was Thinking that the Previous Chapter would be Discussing the Evils of Demon-ocracy, or Mob Rulership, which is only Possible by Election Deceptions, whereby Powerless Presidents are Elected, who make all Kinds of Fake Promises to Fix this or that; but, after they get into their Offices, they seem to Forget what they Promised to Fix. For Example, the Fake Trumpeter was going to Fix the Border Wall from East to West, and make the Mexicans Pay for it; but, only less than 400 Miles of the 1,954 Miles got Worked on, and most of that was already Done before the Fake Trumpeter arrived. Then he Promised to Fix the Infrastructure — the Highways, Bridges, Sewage Systems, Electric Grid, Water Pipes, and Social Security — but, none of that got Fixed. However, he did Manage to Funnel a lot more Money into the Bank Accounts of Rich People by giving to them Tax Breaks. Meanwhile, the Poor People and Homeless People Multiplied by the Millions, along with Police Brutalities, Murders, and Hate Crimes toward "those little brown people from Central America," who only Wanted to Raise their Standards of Living, who were Begging for Tools to Work with.

08-02 [_] Well, my Friend, it was all a Grand Deception of Capitalism, which Tries to take Care of Rich People, and even does a Poor Job of that: beCause the Trumpites got as much or more of the Bug-19 as anyone else. In Fact, I Heard that 47% of the White House Staff contracted it; but, who Cares? It was all of the Victims of Trump's Deceptions, who got the Worst End of the Deal; and it is not nearly over with. Nevertheless, the Hardcore Trumpites are Fully Persuaded that Donald Trump was "the best President in American History." Most of them will likely go down to their Graves Believing it, which is Proof that a large percentage of the People are Vulnerable to Propagandist Lies, and Believe whatever they are Told to Believe. Many of them Believe that the Crotch-grabber is actually a "Christian"! I am wondering which Doctrine of Jesus Christ that he Accepts and Practices? He says that he does not Object to Immigration, just as long as it is done Legally, according to the LAW, which is another Entangled Web of Lies and Deceptions. First of all, the Immigrant must have thousands of Dollars, just to Hire a Lawyer, in Order to get his Legal Papers. Imagine how many Europeans would have gotten in with a Plan like that? Millions of them were so Poor that they went to Work in Sewing Factories in New York City, just to Survive, whereby they Lowered their Standard of Living from that of Normal Europeans. Many of them were made into Slaves in Slaughterhouses in Chicago, which Inspired Upton Sinclair to write a Book, called: *The Jungle,* which Exposed some of the Sins of Capitalism, and even Helped some Poor People; but, did it Fix their Major Problems? Did it Provide Good Health for anyone? Most of that Generation Died with Heart Attacks, Cancers, Diabetes, Strokes, and other Diseases. Oh, but, it is a Wonderful Life, they say! It is so Wonderful that 20,000 or more Commit Suicide, each Year, along with 1 out of 20 Veterans, who were made Extremely Happy by Murdering Innocent People in the Middle East, in the Holy Names of Demon-ocracy, Freedom, Liberty, and Justice for ALL! HUMBUG! Even if they got them Converted to American Capitalism, they would only make them 2-fold more the Children of Hell than they were before: beCause one Satanic False Economy is just as Bad or Worse than the other Satanic False Economy. Why not make a Good Economy for everyone, by getting everyone Set Up Properly for Living on their own Land? It is really a lot more Fun than you can Imagine, when you have your own Animals to Play with. †§‡§§

08-03 [_] O Selected King of **"The New RIGHTEOUS One-World Government,"** if we Followed your Plan, and did our Best to get everyone Set Up Properly for Living on the Land, very few People would Care about Politics: beCause, their Main Concern would be their Fruit Trees and Vegetable Gardens, if they had to Rely on them; but, how many People would have any Idea HOW to Grow any Foods to Eat, seeing that they were never Tawt any such Things in "The Public School of IGNERUNT FQLZ!" (HOW we have been GRAATLEE DISEEVD by Capitalism!) By The Worldwide People's Revolution!® Book 024B? Trust me, they would all be LOST in the Darkness of Ignorance, having no Idea where to Begin their Gardening. Therefore, the First Thing that we would have to Do, is to EDUCATE them! But, they would no doubt not be Interested in Growing any Foods: beCause, it Requires several YEARS to get any Fruits on Trees, and then it Requires Special Nolij to Preserve those Fruits. Therefore, your **"Seven Great Armies of Working Soldiers"** would have to have Good, Honest, Well-Educated School Teachers, who would have to Attend Classes, themselves, just to Learn what to Teach to those Children, who would Naturally be more Ignorant than African Jungle Bunnies, Algaegators and Swamp Rats. †§‡§§

08-04 [_] Well, my Friend, I Know what you are Saying, and it is Frightening! Therefore, it is Best to TRANSITION our Way into it, one Step at a Time: beCause, it could Cause an Economic CRASH, if most People just Quit their Jobs, and went Home and went to Bed with Depression! Indeed, the Right Way to Transition our Way into it, is to Begin to Build those Hotels, just as I already Explained in: "HOW to Conquer the World by Constructing GLORIOUS HOTELS!" (A Peaceful Takeover of the Evil Empires!) **By The Worldwide People's Revolution!®** Book 136, which is a Companion Book of: "The Affordable Constitutional Health Care Act!" (A New Amendment to the Constitution for the United States of North America!) **By The Worldwide People's Revolution!®** Book 137, and: "Would you Vote for Jesus Christ to be your Elected King?" (The Skeptic will say that Jesus Christ would never be Campaigning for any Election Deceptions!) **By The Worldwide People's Revolution!®** Book 139. Study it.

08-05 [_] O Selected King, there would be no Problem at all, if ALL of the People Cheerfully Submitted to YOU: beCause, you could put all of them to Work for Good Swanky Wages, while Constructing those Glorious Swanky Fortresses. However, they would never be Willing to go along with that Plan: beCause, like the Trumpeter, they are SPOILED by their Easy Lifestyles. §‡

08-06 [_] Well, my Friend, X-number of them are Spoiled, and X-number are Drug Addicts, who cannot be Helped, until the Swanky Fortress System gets Established. Therefore, that will Require some Patience. BUT, the entire Generation of Young People, from Ages 10 to 20, are Lined Up Perfect for Working at those Swanky Hotels, who will Need Reliable and Trustworthy Fathers and Mothers to Educate them, who can Adopt them into their Families, if their Parents do not Want to Join us, and many of them will not Want to, which is Okay: beCause we would not Want any Unhappy People to Join us. However, the entire Younger Generation would no doubt Love to Join us: beCause of getting to Eat at those "Royal Swanky Buffets!" (The Best Feasts in the Whole World!) By The Worldwide People's Revolution!® Book 103, and Liv in those "Beautiful Swanky PALACES!" (A New Concept in Living Habits — Swanky Palaces for Poor People!) By The Worldwide People's Revolution!® Book 066. Yes, any 12-year-old Boy would LOVE it, and soon Love his New Adopted Father and Mother, even if they had 20 Children to Care for. After all, someone must Keep those Children Out of Troubles, until they Grow Up into Responsible People. BUT, just HOW to Do that, presents a Controversy, which should be Settled at **"The GWTCH!"** Book 041B.

1 08-07 [_] O Selected King, I Believe that if we Ask for Volunteers, and let them Know what we Need, everything will fall into its Proper Place within a Year or less, and everyone will be Happy with your Master Plan: beCause, all of the Teenage Boys will be Busy Constructing those Swanky Hotels, beginning with the Terraced Cisterns. After all, those Teenagers have an Abundance of Energy to Burn, and they will be Happy to Do it: beCause of being Reminded on a Daily Basis what to Expect when it is all Finished, who will no doubt get Married and Settle Down within their own "Beautiful Swanky Stone Dome Home COMPLEXES!" (HOW to Build SECURE Tax-proof, Insurance-proof, Self-air-conditioned, Paint-proof, Rot-proof, Termite-proof, Mouse-proof, Fireproof, Tornado-proof, Hurricane-proof, Thief-proof, and BOMB-PROOF Houses!) By The Worldwide People's Revolution!® Book 102. Indeed, it is a Lifetime Opportunity that no Young Person could Rightfully Pass Up! However, the Problem will be Keeping those Young People INNOCENT, when they get around the Older Boys and Girls, who have already Learned far too many Evil Ways, who have Lost their Innocence, who are into Fornication, Sodomy, and whatever. Therefore, just HOW to Keep the Children Innocent, is a Major Problem, in my Viewpoint; but, you are Welcome to Send your Suggestions to us. †§‡§§

08-08 [_] Well, my Friend, that is the Reason for having Good, Honest, Reliable PARENTS, who do their Best to Maintain the Innocence of the Children, who Teach them to Pray to God, Sing Hymns, and Study the New MAGNIFIED Versions of the Scriptures, including: "The New MAGNIFIED Version of The Book of MORMON!" (The Story of the White and Dark Indians in the Americas!) By Big Chief Stands Over Bull in the River of Life with a Mile-High Erectile Dysfunction! Book 040. Yes, it Sounds a little "Nasty." But, it is Actually one of the Best Books in the Whole World, which is very Educational. Therefore, anyone who is 12 Years or Older will Greatly Appreciate it. But, first of all, they should Study: "The New MAGNIFIED Version of the PSALMS of King David!" (The Understandable Version of the Famous Psalms in Plain English!) By The Worldwide People's Revolution!® Book 064, "The New MAGNIFIED Version of The GOOD NEWS According to Saint JOHN!" (The Gospel According to Saint John Zebedee Boanerges [pronounced Boo-an-er-jeez] in Plain English!) By The Worldwide People's Revolution!® Book 062, "The New MAGNIFIED Version of The GOOD NEWS According to Saint LUKE!" (The Magnified Gospel of Saint Luke in Plain English!) By The Worldwide People's Revolution!® Book 061, "God Speaks and the Whole World Listens!" (Fire on the Mountain from the Burning Bush by the Spirit of Truths!) By The Worldwide People's Revolution!® Book 026B, "Does a Good Soldier have to be a MURDERER?" (Seven Great Swanky Armies of Voluntary Working Soldiers!) By The Worldwide People's Revolution!® Book 027B, "Thu Nq MAGNUFIID Verzhun uv Thu PROVERBZ uv KING SOLUMUN in Plaan Ingglish!" (The Understandable Version of the Famous Proverbs of King Solomon in Plain English!) By The Worldwide People's Revolution!® Book 028, "SWANGKEENOMIKS Rules the Roost!" (HOW all People can Prosper in a RIIT WAA, and STOP Polluting the Earth with Capitalist TRASH!) By The Worldwide People's Revolution!® Book 039, "The Nature of CAPITALISM!" (A List of the EVILS of CAPITALISM!) By The Worldwide People's Revolution!® Book 038, "The Seven Basic Spiritual Building Blocks of LIFE!" (Faith Hope Trust Love Patience Persistence and Obedience!) By The Worldwide People's Revolution!® Book 036, "The Environmentalists' Perfect Paradise!" (HOW almost Everyone can be Living in a Beautiful Manmade Paradise!) By The Worldwide People's Revolution!® Book 035C, and "ECCLESIASTES Uncovered and Recovered!" (The New MAGNIFIED Version of Ecclesiastes and the Song of Solomon in Plain English!) By The Worldwide People's Revolution!® Book 034.

1 08-09 [_] O Selected King, by the Time those Teenagers get Finished with Reeding all of those
2 Books, they will be Spiritually-Old Well-Seasoned Adults, if they just have Loving Parents to
3 Answer their Important Questions, who should be Monitored by "The New RIGHTEOUS One-
4 World Government," which would have to Listen in on every Classroom. Therefore, I Suggest
5 that everyone in the World should get the same Exact Lessons at the same Time of the Day, every
6 Day, whereby they are all on the same Page of the same Book, you might say. †‡

8 08-10 [_] Well, my Friend, that Sounds Good — except that there are 10,000 or more
9 Contradictory Religions, which will all have to be Proven to be WRong at "The GREAT
10 Worldwide TELEVISED Court HEARING!" Book 041B, whereby they can all Agree to Teach
11 the same Provable Truths, which is Asking for more than Humanity can Deliver, I would say. †§‡

— Chapter 09 —

We still Look for the Second Coming of Jesus Christ!

18 09-01 [_] Readers must Remember that I have only come to Prepare the Way for the Second
19 Coming of Jesus Christ — not to Replace him, as some People might Vainly Imagine: beCause,
20 there is no Way that I could ever Replace him: beCause, he has the Experiences of many Lifetimes
21 in many Worlds, while I am just a "Baby Christian," you might say, who has a LOT to Learn. †§‡

23 09-02 [_] O Selected King, I Hope that Jesus will be a bit more Organized than you are. But, after
24 reading your New MAGNIFIED Versions of the *Scriptures,* I am not Sure that such a Thing is
25 Possible: beCause, it is Well Organized, and much Better than I could ever Do. In Fact, I have no
26 Idea how that you could Write an Inspired Book every Week, which is a World Record and a Feat
27 that Challenges any other Author, who might write a book during one Month, or one Year; but,
28 certainly not a Book every Week for several Months, or even for several Years, which is Proof
29 that you are Inspired by some God, or Devil. However, why would Satan be Interested in putting
30 himself Out of Business, by Revealing Provable Truths? I Think that would be Irrational. †§‡§§

32 09-03 [_] Well, my Friend, there is always the Possibility that Satan is making "a Last-Ditch
33 Struggle to Lead the entire World into a Peacock TRAP," as one of my Critics put it. However,
34 could a Man be Setting a Trap that he knows nothing about? What would be the Purpose for the
35 Trap? What would be the Trap? It makes no Sense to me. Indeed, I have been Thinking that I have
36 come to Liberate People from the Pits and Traps that they are already in, whereby they are all
37 Slaves of Various Kinds, which can easily be Proven in a Courtroom, if anyone Doubts it.
38 However, my Enemies Suggest that I am Seeking to Enslave everyone, without Explaining their
39 False Accusations. Whose Slaves would they be? Who would the Slave Masters be, if everyone
40 has his own Private Garden of Eden to Liv in? Some People say that it is Physically Impossible
41 for the Working Soldiers to Accomplish enough Work within only 4 Hours of Common Skilled
42 Labor per Workday, to get everyone Moderately Rich: beCause they could never Do enough Work
43 by Hand. However, I am not Against the Use of Mechanical Slaves, if the Working Soldiers Want
44 to Use them: beCause, that will be their Decision. In Fact, I Strongly Suggest that they Wisely Use
45 all such Mechanical Slaves for the Construction of Swanky Fortresses, just to SPEED UP the

1 Process, and Hopefully Win the Race with Climate Changes, before it becomes Unbearably HOT
2 and Miserable to Do any Work Outside. After all, just the Air-conditioners, alone, will be Raising
3 the Earth's Temperature, which will be Calling for more and MORE Air-Conditioners, just to Keep
4 everyone Comfortable. Indeed, it will be like Ciudad Bolivar in the Gran Savana of Venezuela,
5 where the Hotel Rooms do not Cool Off enough to Sleep Well, in spite of Running 24/7/365! But,
6 if you Drink a couple very Cold Beers, you can get a little Sleep. But, the Outside Temperature is
7 almost Unbearable by 9 a.m. Nevertheless, many People Liv there: beCause, there is Work that
8 Needs Doing, and the Slave-labor Wages are a little Better than in other Places, where it is more
9 Comfortable and Livable. However, the People who were Born and Raised there, have gotten Used
10 to it, and can Tolerate it; but, they cannot Tolerate Cold Climates, as I might, being a White Man.

12 09-04 [_] O Selected King, I Think that Fearful People are Worried about Changing their Lifestyles
13 in a Dramatic Way, which they are not Used to, which has them Scared half to Death, in spite of
14 the Fact that there is nothing to be Greatly Concerned about: beCause, most People Lived on the
15 Land for thousands of Years, including our own Forefathers — such as George Prayer Book
16 Washington and Saint Thomas Jefferson, who had their Slaves to Help them; but, they also did a
17 lot of Manual Labor, themselves: beCause, they Felt Good by Working for a Living. It was FUN!

19 09-05 [_] Well, my Friend, when you only do 4 Hours of Work per Workday, you soon get Used
20 to it, and do not Fear it. The Army often puts in 16 Hours per Day, and we had some 20-Hours-
21 per-Day in Vietnam, and a few 22-Hour Days; but, none of it was Necessary. They just Needed to
22 have more Men, whereby they could have Spread Out the Work among them. After all, the Beds
23 were Empty for most of the Day, which could have been Occupied by Sleeping Soldiers. †§‡

25 09-06 [_] O Selected King, the Army has Traditionally been Short on Men and Money, and Long
26 on Labor and Complaints. Here is a YouTube Video, called: **Bitter Chocolate | DW**
27 **Documentary,** https://youtu.be/pRwMoGPTEEM which is about the Exploitation of Children
28 on Cocoa Farms, which is a Perfect Example of Capitalism at its Best. It has gotten 381,973 Views,
29 as of September 28, 2020. So, if you like to Eat Chocolate, that Video is just for YOU. Enjoy! †§‡

31 09-07 [_] Well, my Friend, it has been several Years since I Ate any Chocolate, in spite of Hearing
32 that it is supposed to be Good for us to Eat, which is supposed to make our Brains Function Better.

34 09-08 [_] O Selected King, I would say that People, who like to Exploit Children, and make Slaves
35 of them, do not have Functioning Brains, at all, who should be Born in Africa, the next Time
36 Around, just to get a Taste of Slavery. Nevertheless, what is to be Done about it, to Straighten Out
37 that Exploitation? Will **"The New RIGHTEOUS One-World Government"** be Able to Handle
38 it, and Correct it? Or, will their Sex-addicted "Leaders" be Exploiting the Children, also? †§‡§§

40 09-09 [_] Well, my Friend, that Government cannot be any Better than the People in Charge of it.
41 Therefore, every Potential Member should have to Fill Out and File: **"The Complete SURVEYS**
42 **of our VALUES!" (SURVEYS of Religious Spiritual Political Governmental Sexual Social**
43 **Moral Economical Business Labor Habitual and Miscellaneous VALUES!) By The**
44 **Worldwide People's Revolution!®** Book 059, which the Electors can Study on the Internet,
45 before Voting for them to Govern them, which may not Fix all such Problems; but, at least it will
46 Help to Fix them, and will also Help to Discover other Righteous People to Vote for. †§‡

09-10 [_] O Selected King, you can Adopt the Good Name of King David, and we Electors will Vote for you to be our Righteous King; but, the Problem is, you will soon Die, and leave us with the same Problem. Therefore, how can we Fix that Problem?

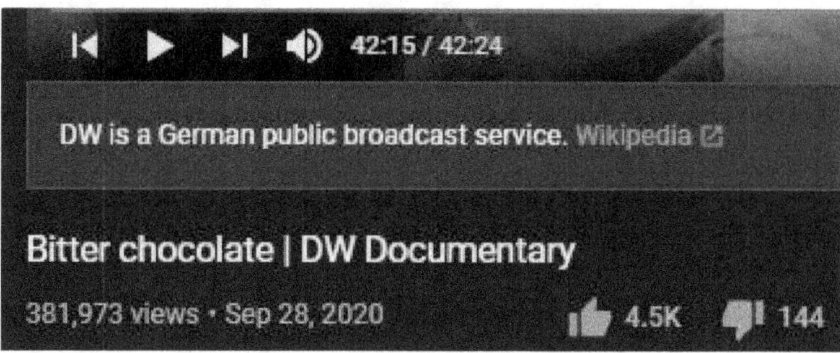

— Chapter 10 —

The Conclusion

10-01 [_] This has got to be my Weirdest Book, which is almost as Weird as the *Old Testament,* when Addressing the Future of Israel, which makes little or no Sense, at all. But, the Words are arranged in a Way that they can be Misinterpreted in a thousand different ways, whereby there can be 10,000 Contrary Beliefs, which makes one wonder if they are Prophecies or just Islamic-type Meaningless Blabbering, like the Unholy Repetitious Koran, which makes a Person Sick? †§‡§§

10-02 [_] Do the People of the World Deserve a Righteous King to Govern them? Do they Care about Righteousness? Do they Care about Solving their Problems? Are they on some Strange Mass-Suicide Mission? Are they in a Worse Mental Condition than those Sick Republicans, who Telephone the *Washington Journal,* on the C-SPAN Network, who have never Red "The Washington Journal is a FARCE! (C-SPAN Managers are not very WISE!) By The Worldwide People's Revolution!® Book 006C? Of course, the Most-Intelligent People would not be Calling the *Washington Journal:* beCause they would Realize that they are only Talking to a Mob of mostly Ignorant, Self-Deceived Fools, who only Want their Voices to be HEARD, who have no **"Guaranteed Solutions"** to Offer to anyone, who might Ask: "How would the Construction of Swanky Fortresses Solve our Problems, which are Rooted in the Love of Money — not in Obtaining a Peaceful Garden of Eden Lifestyle?" In Fact, they have no Desires at all for a Garden of Eden Lifestyle, which is Suggesting that they might have to Bend Over and Plants some Seeds in a Garden, which is away Below their Dignity, even though George Beverley Shea did it for most of his Life, and he Lived for 104 Years, and was still Singing like a Canary! Yes, they would rather Beg for Handouts at Soup Kitchens, and Stand in such Long Lines all Day Long, just to get a little Bowl of Insipid Soup, Oversalted Soup, Burnt Stew, or Dog Meat. Who would Know for Sure what is in the Kettle? Maybe it is Parts from the Victims of the Bug-19? Maybe it is Horse Meat, Ground up Mule Meat, or Recycled Dog Food? Who would Know? Take a Guess.

10-03 [_] O Selected King, if you do not get any Feedback from your Readers, how will you ever Know what they are Thinking? Are they all Thinking the same Things? Have their Minds been

Trained to NOT Think? Whatever Happened to Reason and Logic? Why would they not Prefer to Liv in *"The IDEAL Place to Live!" (HOW to Discover the Ideal Place to Live!) By The Worldwide People's Revolution!®* Book 069? Why do they Prefer to Suffer, than to be Healthy, Wealthy and Wise? Indeed, it Reminds me of a Verse in *Amos 5:13, "Therefore, the Prudent People will Keep Silent during that Time: beCause, it is an Evil Time."* For Sure, God keeps …

10-04 [_] Well, my Friend, I must say that it is very Depressing when there is no Encouragement from anyone. Am I supposed to Liv on Ancient Sayings, Foolish Proverbs, Book of Mormon Deceptions, and Islamic Nonsense? How in the World could a Billion People fall for such Nonsense? What do they get out of it? It is like, *"Hail Mary, Mother of God, the LORD be with thee!"* Why did she not write a book of some kind, just to let us know what the LORD had to Tell her during those Secret Meetings? Maybe it would have been Helpful during Depressing Times? (Most People do not know that the Apostle Paul wrote his Epistles BEFORE any of the Gospels were written; but, that Explains a few Mysteries and Contradictions, which Luke tried to Correct.)

10-05 [_] O Selected King, I just Happen to Liv in a House with a Crazy Woman in Charge of it, who has 2 Teenage Children, and all 3 of them cannot Manage to keep the Water Tank on the Roof full of Water, in spite of only having to Turn On the Pump, and Fill Up the Tank before going to Bed, which Requires all of 10 Minutes of Patience. The Mother Forbids the Children to Fill Up the Tank before Bedtime: beCause, she is Worried that it might Run Out of Water, if it is Filled Up at 4 p.m., instead of 9:30. Therefore, once or twice a Week, they Forget to Fill Up the Tank, and sure enough, it runs Dry, and loses its Pressure, and then there is no Water in the House, until they go to the Trouble to Connect a Hose to the Pipe, and Force Water through it, which is a lot more Trouble than just Turning On the Pump, once per Day, and Walking Up the Steps to Check on the Fulness of the Water Tank, which might Require all of 1 Minute, or 2 at the most. Indeed, the Son would not Object to Doing it, each Day, and be Responsible for Doing it; but, the Crazy B**** will not give to him the Responsibility of Taking Care of it. No one can figure out what her Problem is. However, it seems like she only Wants to Torment her Husband, who gets Pissed Off when there is no Water in the Toilet to Flush it, who would Like to Strap her Fat Ass; but, someone would say that he is Beating on her, and that she should Divorce him for it, and Collect Alimony. However, that is no Good Solution. Why not just Kindly Ask her Son to take Responsibility for Keeping the Water Tank Full of Water, or else Strap his Fat Ass? After all, he is not Stupid; but, she is about as Stupid as Women come, who puts Pots of Water on the Gas Stove without Lids on them, and Turns the Gas on HIGH, and Heats Up the entire House in the Middle of Summer, and then Turns On the Air-conditioner to Cool Off, while her Husband is Expected to Pay the Electric Bills, which are like 300$ per Month, while the Gas Bill is like 150$ per Month during the Summer, and 350$ during the Winter, which could be Zero Dollars, if they Lived within a Swanky Fortress.

10-06 [_] Well, my Friend, such Stupid People would likely leave the Doors and Windows Wide Open all Night, when the Outside Temperature is Minus 20 Degrees Fahrenheit: beCause, they do not Use their Heads to Think, nor Remember anything, who Need a Good Whipping with the Bug-19, or some other Bug, whereby they might come to their Riit Senses. Why not put the Gas Burner on the Lowest Amount of Heat, and put a Lid on the Kettle, and Save as much Gas as Possible, rather than Heat Up the Whole House with it? Is it Laziness, Craziness, or a Deliberate Plot to make Enemies with her Husband? What Kind of a Demon Spirit Possesses her? The Water in a Good Kettle can be brought to a Boil on a Gas Stove in 5 to 15 Minutes, depending on the

1 Temperature of the Water and the House, as well as the Amount of Water, which can be Timed on
2 a Clock, whereby it can be Closely Calculated each Time that she Cooks the Beans, whereby very
3 little Gas would have to be Wasted. Indeed, a hundred Gallons of Propane should Last a Family at
4 least a Year to do the Cooking, if it is Used Wisely; but, some Women simply do not Care how
5 much Gas they Waste, nor if they Drive their Husbands Crazy over it. Chances are that they will
6 be Born in Haiti, the next Time Around, where they have nothing to Work with. Should we Feel
7 Sorry for them? Were they so-called "Rich People" during their Previous Lives? Would they
8 Believe it, even if God Told them so? What is God supposed to Do to Correct them? How could
9 he Correct such Stupid People? The Hurricanes come on a Regular Basis, and Blow Down their
10 Shanties, and they just Build more of them, instead of figuring out how to use their Rocks to Build
11 with. After all, a Concrete Roof is Cheaper than a Tin Roof, in the Long Run. Nearly every
12 Mexican House has a Concrete Roof. Some are Tiled with Ceramic Tiles, which keeps the
13 Rainwater from Rusting Out the Steel Reinforcement Bars in the Concrete Roof, whereby it might
14 Endure for 200 or more Years; but, the Poor Person cannot Afford the Ceramic Tiles, in spite of
15 the Fact that he can Afford to Drink Beers every Weekend, while his Wife Gathers Sticks and Dry
16 Weeds for Cooking her Beans and Tortillas. It is all Insanity: beCause, they could have an
17 Unlimited Supply of ElecTrickery, if they Followed my Plan, which would Require some Work;
18 but, not nearly as much Work as going to the Mountains to Gather some Sticks to Pack Home on
19 their Backs; or, on the Backs of their Burros. I say, it is all CRAZY! Why not Demand a Righteous
20 One-World Government, and get everyone Set Up Properly for Living, and Teach the Children
21 HOW to Manage themselves Properly, and be Done with the Nonsense? Why should Poor People
22 not have Gardens? Why should the Topsoil not be Protected by Solid Stone Walls, which can also
23 Keep Out the Unwanted Varmints? Indeed, if God had not Provided every Good Thing to Work
24 with, we might have Good Excuses for not Doing it Properly; but, Thank God, he Provided
25 everything that is Necessary for True Prosperity, at HOME, O Fools! Indeed, you might have to
26 Play around in the Garden every Day or 2, for 10 to 20 Minutes, just to keep the Weeds under
27 Control; but, that would b a lot less Effort than getting Up at 4 a.m. to Fix Breakfast and Lunch in
28 a Box, and Drive for 2 Hours in Traffic Jams, just to Maintain some Boring Job in the City of
29 Confusion, when you could be at Home, Playing with your Children, or Playing in your Home-
30 craft Workshop, making some Special Furniture, Clothes, Shoes, or something. Indeed, they did it
31 for thousands of Years, and no one ever Heard of a Divorce, nor Suicide. My Grandfather was the
32 first Person in our Family to Hear about anyone in the Family Dying with Cancer. None of his
33 Friends nor Relatives ever Died with Cancer. In Fact, if they Lived long enough to Grow Up, they
34 almost all Lived to be Old and Happy. The same was True of the American Indians. Many of them
35 Lived to be 100 or more, and did not Die with Cancers. BUT, then came the Industrial Revolution,
36 along with the Pesticides, Herbicides, Chemical Fertilizers, Chemical Perfumes, Plastic Trash,
37 Artificial Sweeteners, Refined Sugar, Candy Bars, Cokes, and an entire List of Abominations,
38 which Adam and Eve Lived for 900 Years without, and were Happy with their Lifestyle. †§‡§§
39
40 10-07 [_] O Selected King, there is no Going Back to "the Good Old Days": beCause, they are
41 Gone Forever. The Earth has been Ruined by Capitalism, and most People are Happy with their
42 Sicknesses and Diseases: beCause they have Magic Pills that Kill their Pains and Deaden their
43 Brains. Therefore, just leave them to Suffer as much as they Like: beCause, they are CRAZY! §§
44
45 10-08 [_] Well, my Friend, I Wanted to Help them to be Saved from their Madness, and I Wrote
46 140 Good Books for that Reason; but, it seems that it was all just a Waste of my Precious Time.

Therefore, I must Dedicate this next Year to Fasting and Praying for them. Perhaps God will have Mercy on us, and Transform some Rough Rocks into Pure Gold, whereby I can get their Attention?

10-09 [_] O Selected King of **The Worldwide People's Revolution,** if you do not get put in Charge of Things around here, it is all likely to End with "The Great ATOMIC NIGHTMARE!" (The Saddest Story in World History!) By The Great White Bald Eagle! Book 099. After all, you are Correct — that they are CRAZY, Insane IDIOTS, who cannot Agree with Reason nor Logic, who Vainly Believe that Good Health comes with Drugs, Countless Pills and Endless Bills! Therefore, what can be Done for them? They are a Lost Generation of Ignorant MORONS! †§‡§§

10-10 [_] Well, my Friend, there is still one more Option, which is Explained in: "What will you Do when the Rain STOPS?" (God's Last Resort to Save Mankind from his MADNESS!) By The Worldwide People's Revolution!® Book 101. Yes, when their Bellybuttons are Rubbing on their Backbones for Hunger and Thirst, they will have Time to Think about getting their Priorities in Order, and might even Study: "HOW to Get our PRIORITIES in ORDER!" (The Glories of Democracy; and, Does DEMON-ocracy have its Priorities in Order?) By The Worldwide People's Revolution!® Book 060. But, being Poor, they could never Afford any such Books, unless they had enough Common Sense to POOL their Resources, in Order to Buy ALL of the Books, and then put them into their Church Library, or even into their Public LIE-brary, and then SHARE them with one another from their Church Truth-brary, at Home, after they Learn HOW to Save Money by Good Self-Discipline, just by Eating less, as well as simple, unprocessed Foods. My Brother Vern and I Lived for at least 5 Years, on only 400$ per Month, and did not Starve. Of course, we did not Visit any Medical Snakes, nor Consume any Pills, nor Pay any Bills; but, that was only beCause of being Set Up Properly for Living, at Home, in a Blest Land with no Taxes! †§‡§§

— Chapter 40 —

A Long List of other Fascinating Literature by the same Inspired Author!

[_] 40-001 — "LIGHTNING **Versus the** Lightning Bug!" (HOW almost Everyone can become Moderately RICH, without Telling Any Lies nor Selling Any Capitalist Trash!) By The Worldwide People's Revolution!® Book 001B. There are several Books with similar Titles, which are all Different and Unique. See Books 072, 073, and 074.

[_] 40-002 — "What is WRong with those Professing Christians?" (A Self-Examination of the Heart of the Body of Good Government!) By The Worldwide People's Revolution!® Book 002B. This is a Companion Book of: "What is WRong with those CRAZY CHRISTIANS?" (A Self-Examination of the Heart of the Body of Good Government!) By The Worldwide People's Revolution!® Book 076, which contains many Photographs with Enlightening Explanations. They moved 66,666,666 Pounds by Hand to Build their Unique Retirement Home in the Blest Land of Eternal Springtime!

[_] 40-003 — "For the Love of Money!" (The Strange Things that People Say and Do to Get more Money!) By The Worldwide People's Revolution!® Book 003B. This is a Twin Companion Book of: "The Root Cause for almost all Evils!" (The Strange Things that People Say and Do to Get more Money!) By The Worldwide People's Revolution!® Book 078. It is NOT an Identical Twin Companion Book, however; but, just a Beautiful Twin. You will Love both Books, if you Reed them Carefully. (And "Reed" is speld Funetiklee, which makes it Kurekt, or Koor-rekt at the Core of it.)

14

15

[_] 40-004 — "How Best to Prepare for CLIMATE CHANGES!" (The Wisest Plan for Mankind to Follow!) By The Worldwide People's Revolution!® Book 004B. This is a Companion Book of: "UNLIMITED ENERGY 99 Percent Pollution-Free!" (HOW to Obtain Free ElecTrickery, Worldwide!) By The Worldwide People's Revolution!® Book 029B. Do not Miss Out on the Greatest Idea since the Invention of the Light Bulb! Get Prepared for the Worst Living Conditions: beCause, they are Bound to Come, O Lady Doubtfulness!

29

[_] 40-005 — "Why do I have to be Surrounded by CRAZY PEOPLE!" (Do almost all People Feel like they are Surrounded by CRAZY People?) By The Worldwide People's Revolution!® Book 005B. Just Think — if you Ordered those 2 White Boys to go Roll around in the Mud with the Hogs, all Day long, they would just Naturally REFUSE; but, give to them the Freedom to make Fools of themselves, and they will have Fun doing it all Day long! WHY is that? Could Voluntary Working Soldiers have a lot more Fun, without Rolling around in the Mud of Conceit with J. Edgar Whomever and Beardless Josephine Biden, Junior? Lighten Up, O Crocodiles and Algaegators: beCause, there is Plenty of Space in the Swamp for all of you Beardless Sissies and Spiritual Cowards. (See *Leviticus 19:15—16, and 27; 21:5; Isaiah 15:2; Jeremiah 16:6; Ezekiel 7:18; KJV.*)

[_] 40-006 — "The Washington Journal is a FARCE! (C-SPAN Managers are not very WISE!) By The Worldwide People's Revolution!® Book 006C. (This Book has lots of Good Humor, and comes in 5 Different Editions at different Prices See Amazon.com.)

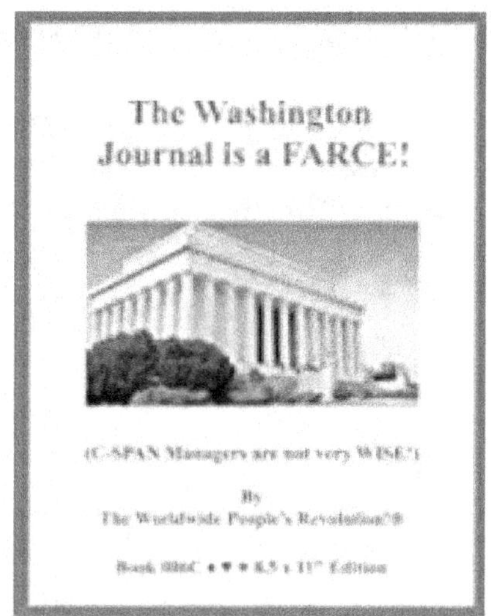

[_] 40-007 — "The PRAYERS of PUMPKINHEADS!" (This Book is otherwise known as the Prayers of Preachers, Priests, Professors, Politicians, Prostitutes, Policemen, Pumpkinheads, Punks, Prisoners, and other Professionals — in other Words, the Capital P People!) By The Worldwide People's Revolution!® Book 007B. (Some of it is for Adults only, and mostly for Men.)

[ ] 40-008 — "A Sound Argument for Good Masters and Obedient Servants!" (WHY Everyone Needs a Good Master, and every Master Needs Good Obedient Servants!) By The Worldwide People's Revolution!® Book 008B. This Book contains the KEY that can be Used Wisely for Unlocking the Door on the Prison of Lies, whereby Humanity can Escape from all of its Curses and Woes, just by having some Righteous Men in Charge! See: "Our Selected King SPEAKS OUT!" (It is High Time for some Sane Person to get Total Control of this Insane World!) By The Worldwide People's Revolution!® Book 100. The "Secret" to Success is becoming the King of your own Swanky Castle. See: "GOVERNMENT Versus Independence!" (How Much CONTROL Should a Government Have?") By The Worldwide People's Revolution!® Book 096.

15

16

[ ] 40-009 — "WHY are some Preachers so POOR?" (HOW almost all Preachers can Get Moderately RICH, without Preaching any Outlandish LIES!) By The Worldwide People's Revolution!® Book 009B. Priests and Preachers should be Paid Well to Preach the Truth, even if no one Likes it: beCause, our Salvation from our Sins and Troubles is Depending on it. Therefore, they should not have to Liv on Free-will Contributions nor Donations of any Kind; but, they should be Well Cared for by the Federal Government, even as Moses Tawt, whereby they will not be Afraid to Speak Truths to Powerful Governments of Satan, the Devil, who has Ordained them for his own Selfish Purposes. In Fact, a Lack of Truths is the Downfall of any Nation. Therefore, this is one of the most Important Books.

30

[ ] 40-010 — "GOOD NEWS for REBEL WOMEN!" (HOW almost all Wives can become Moderately RICH without Leaving their Homes! Guaranteed!) By The Worldwide People's Revolution!® Book 010B. This is a Companion Book of: "Has your Life become Extremely Complicated?" (HOW to Live a SIMPLE Life!) By The Worldwide People's Revolution!® Book 068. See also: "How all Women can Get True Justice without Getting Divorced from God!" (The Unjust Case of Judge Brett Kavanaugh and Doctor Christine Blasey Ford is now Revisited by a Wise Son of King Solomon!) By The Worldwide People's Revolution!® Book 087. It will likely Surprise you, even as Provable Truths have Surprised most People in this World of Woes: beCause, the Truth is often the Opposite of whatever we have been Tawt to Believe!

45

1

16

[_] 40-011 — "The Low Court of Supreme Injustices is Brought to Trial!" (Our Selected King Butts Heads with the United States Supreme Court, with or without their Black Robes of Hypocrisies and Lies!) By The Worldwide People's Revolution!® Book 011B. {This Inspired Book contains the Famous *Declaration of Interdependence,* which is a Must-Reed Book with a Lot of Provable Truths. It also contains the Correct Wording for the Placard on the Statue of Liberty. You will likely Want to Post it on your own Front Door, which is Okay with God and all Honest Righteous People; but, it is not Okay with the Low Court of Supreme Injustices, who would find it "Bad for Business": beCause of "The Nature of CAPITALISM!" (A List of the EVILS of CAPITALISM!) By The Worldwide People's Revolution!® Book 038.}

[_] 40-012 — "The Right Design for Living!" (A List of Great Advantages for Building Beautiful Planned City States!) By The Worldwide People's Revolution!® Book 012B. {This Book contains many Important Drawings, as well as HOW to Save hundreds of Trillions of Dollars by Building Swanky Fortresses, and Living in Peace within them. It is a Companion Book of Book 011B, which contains many more Great Advantages for Swanky Fortresses. This is also a Twin Companion Book of: "GLORIOUS Swanky Hotels Castles and Fortresses!" (Beautiful Planned City States for WISE Intelligent Well-Educated People with Common Sense and Good Understanding!) By The Worldwide People's Revolution!® Book 019B; but, it is NOT an Exact Twin, in spite of Looking somewhat Alike on the Front Cover, which has the same Exact Drawings: beCause, it is Appropriate for it.}

31

32

[_] 40-013 — **"The Gospel According to The Worldwide People's Revolution!®" (The Good News from the Most Modern Perspective!)** See Book 077. (This Book contains the Famous Sermon of Jonah to the Ninevites, whereby 120,000 People Repented in Ashes, being Covered with Sackcloth! Do not Miss Out on it. Not even the Rev. Dr. Billy Graham got 120,000 Converts during one Day! Actually, in Reality, he never got so much as ONE True Convert during his entire Life! Yes, it is Proven within Book 083. And that is what is WRong with this Crazy World! The Devil has simply Deceived the Masses of Ignorant People, including yourselves, O Professing "Christians," who are still Sinning! See *James 4:17; Luke 10:22 and Revelation 2:17.* Do you have your White Stone? NO!)

[ ] 40-014 — "Poverty Hunger Riots Strikes Police Brutalities Election Deceptions and Civil Wars!" (The High Price that we Earthlings have Paid for Leaving the Good Land!) By The Worldwide People's Revolution!® Book 014B. {We all have a LOT of Important Things to Learn before we Die, which is what this Life is all about — Learning Good Lessons. However, we cannot Learn those Things with our Heads Stuck in the Proverbial Sand Dune of Worldly Philosophies. Only the Whole Truth can Liberate us, including the Truth about Living in *the Garden of Eden*. This Book is also a Companion Book of: "Has your Life become Extremely Complicated?" (HOW to Live a SIMPLE Life!) By The Worldwide People's Revolution!® Book 068. Trust the Words of God. You can Raise your Standard of Living by many Times!}

14
15

[ ] 40-015 — "Seven Great Armies of Working Soldiers!" (HOW to Provide a Way for Everyone to WORK: so as to Eliminate Poverty, Crimes, Drug Abuses, Prisons and Unnecessary Taxes!) By The Worldwide People's Revolution!® Book 015B. {This Book contains a True-Life Story when the Author was in the Army. It was a Necessary Experience for Learning Good Lessons. Do not Deprive yourself of it. This is one of the Best Books in the Whole World; and none of those Working Soldiers will be Feeling Guilty for Murdering anyone, such as Osama bin Laden, who should have been Arrested and brought to Trial, if he was Guilty of anything. See: "Conspiracy Theories did it!" (The Evil Events of September 11th 2001 are Revisited by a Wise Son of King Solomon!) By The Worldwide People's Revolution!® Book 128.}

29

[ ] 40-016 — "The CONSTITUTION for the New RIGHTEOUS One-World Government!" (HOW all Peoples can get True Justice, and Celebrate the Great Year of JUBILEE!) By The Worldwide People's Revolution!® Book 016B. Are you Afraid of it? WHY? See: "The New RIGHTEOUS One-World Government UPDATED!" Book 056B. There are more than "101 Good Reasons and Great Advantages for Establishing a Righteous One-World Government!" (Government By the People, Of the People, and For the People!) By The Worldwide People's Revolution!® Book 104. Therefore, do not be Afraid of it. Just Study it to Increase your Faith in it, and get Ready for the Second Coming of Jesus Christ: beCause "King David Lives Again!" (WHY Americans, and the Wise People of the Whole World, Want a Righteous KING to Govern them!) By The

44   Worldwide People's Revolution!® Book 142!

15

16

[ ] 40-017 — "The Great World TEMPLE of PEACE!" (The Glory of Jerusalem Arises Again in the Great State of Flexible Texas!) By The Worldwide People's Revolution!® Book 017B. It will be the HEADQUARTERS for: "The New RIGHTEOUS One-World Government!" (HOW to Establish a Righteous One-World Government without Going to WAR!) By The Worldwide People's Revolution!® Book 056. Therefore, have Faith in it, O Lady Doubtfulness: beCause, what will be, will be; and we cannot Change it, except to make it Better or Worse. Why not be Wise and Help each other to make it Better? Put your Trust in God, and Do what is Riit for yourself and others. See: "101 Good Reasons and Great Advantages for Establishing a Righteous One-World Government!" (Government By the People, Of the People, and For the People!) By The Worldwide People's Revolution!® B-104

31

[ ] 40-018 — "The Swanky Associations of Working Soldiers!" (A Fascinating Collection of Various Kinds of Voluntary Working Soldiers!) By The Worldwide People's Revolution!® Book 018B. {There will be thousands of Associations for all Kinds of Occupations, which will Specialize in Fine Arts — such as Hand-carved Leather-bound Books. See "LIGHTNING STRIKES Versus Lightning Bugs!" (HOW you can Become Moderately RICH, without Telling any Lies nor Selling any Trash!) By The Worldwide People's Revolution!® Book 074, for a full-page Picture of a Good Example of such a Beautiful Hand-carved Book Cover. Not surprisingly, it is also found in other Books for Encouragement.}

46

[ ] 40-019 — "GLORIOUS Swanky Hotels Castles and Fortresses!" (Beautiful Planned City States for WISE Intelligent Well-Educated People with Common Sense and Good Understanding!) By The Worldwide People's Revolution!® Book 019B. {This Book contains many Rough Drawings, which could be Greatly Improved upon by someone who Knows the Art, and has the Correct Computer Programs for doing it. "I am too Poor, too Old, and far too Tired to Handle it, all alone," says our Selected King. "You People will have to Help me, and in a BIG Way. I am Relying on you." This is a Companion Book of: "The Right Design for Living!" (A List of Great Advantages for Building Beautiful Planned City States!) By The Worldwide People's Revolution!® Book 012B. Each Book is Unique and Special, in spite of containing similar Ideas, which are Told in Different Ways for Enlightenment.}

[_] 40-020 — "Are you a Jobless Graduate of the SKQL uv FQLZ?" (HOW to Get a GOUD EJUKAASHUN without Robbing the Bank!) By The Worldwide People's Revolution!® Book 020B. (This Inspired Book contains the New MAGNIFIED Version {NMV} of *First Corinthians 13,* plus: HOW to Produce Pure Living Water! You have most likely never Tasted of Living Water, much less, Drink a half-gallon of it, and Feel Really Good from Head to Toe! It Requires a Tall Waterfalls, just to make it! There are only a few Places in this World where it is Found Naturally — such as the Neuschwanstein Castle in Southern Bavaria, in Germany, at the Foot of the Mountain, not too far from the other Castle of King Ludwig II. It is Worth the Trip, just to get a Good Drink of it. Another Place is in Banff National Park, in Canada. But, why not have it at Home?

15

[_] 40-021 — "The LUSCIOUS All-Mineral Organic Method of Gardening!" (HOW to Grow DELICIOUS Satisfying Foods for Potential Kingz and Kweenz in Beautiful Swanky PALACES!) By The Worldwide People's Revolution!® Book 021B. {This Book Explains HOW to make a Flood-proof Garden, while Trapping the Rainwater. As far as we know, no one else has ever Presented this Good Plan. This is a Companion Book of "Orgimmick Gardening at its Best!" (HOW to Grow Delicious Satisfying Foods without a 10 Million-Dollar Investment!) By The Worldwide People's Revolution!® Book 079, and: "Profitable Swanky MULCHING ROCKS!" (30 Advantages for Using Swanky Mulching Rocks in an All-Mineral Organic Garden!) By The Worldwide People's Revolution!® Book 098.}

29

[_] 40-022 — "Did God or Satan Ordain Medical Doctors?" (Ask Huck Finn and/or Nigger Jim: because neither Tom Sawyer nor Judge Thatcher would Know!) By The Worldwide People's Revolution!® Book 022B. {This Inspired Book Reveals HOW to Prevent Common Colds, and has a Special Chapter that Explains what a True "Nigger" IS. Surprise yourself! The World is Full of them! The Fake Trumpeter is one of them! All Wild Animals have only ONE Remedy for whatever Ails them, which is Revealed within this Amazing Book, which is a Companion Book of: "The Proper RULES for FASTING!" (The Complete Instruction Manual for True Repentance!) By The Worldwide People's Revolution!® Book 046, and: "HOW to Become a HOLY Man!" (40 Good Reasons WHY People Should FAST and PRAY!) By The Worldwide People's Revolution!® Book 045. Do not be Afraid of

44
45
it; but, Learn, Believe, Love and OBEY your own Body, which is Smarter than you might Think!}

[_] 40-023 — "The BIG White OUTHOUSE on the Not-so-Biblical Capitol DUNGHILL!" (The Chief Sins of the Divided States of United Lies!) By The Worldwide People's Revolution!® Book 023B. {This Inspired Book contains Special Words that most People have never Heard! Surprise yourself again! For Example, what do you suppose is the single Most-Evil, VILE and Sinful Thing in the Eyes of God, which is Practiced on a Grand Scale in "The Divided States of United Lies!" (The so-called "United States of North America" in Disguise!) By The Worldwide People's Revolution!® Book 058? You will no doubt be Amazed by the Truth of it, O Frogs! It is Time to Move OUT of the Proverbial Swamp, O Chickens!}

[_] 40-024 — "The Public School of IGNERUNT FQLZ!" (HOW we have been GRAATLEE DISEEVD by Capitalism!) By The Worldwide People's Revolution!® Book 024B. {This Book Teaches Children HOW to "Reed and Riit in Swanky Funetik Ingglish in just wun Daa!" You should Challenge your Frendz, Enemies, Relatives and Naaberz with it, who would Naturally not Believe that they could Learn HOW to Spell every Word in the English Language, in just ONE Day! Some of the Smarter 8 to 13-year-old Children can Learn it in less than 15 Minutes. Therefore, why is one-fourth of American Adults unable to read and write as well as Huck Finn? Even Poor "Nigger Jim" can Lern it within a Day or 3, if he is not Mentally Challenged by his own Tally Whacker. His own Aunt Wretched and Uncle Miserable will Agree with us.}

[_] 40-025 — "In thu Beeginingz uv Thingz!" (Thu Kreeaashun Stooree frum thu Beegining!) By The Worldwide People's Revolution!® Book 025B. {The Original Cover Photo showed a Picture of a Golden Supootaa (Sapote), which not one Person in a Million has ever Tasted: because it does not Ship very well, in spite of it being one of the most Sweetest Pleasant Fruits known to Mankind, which must Ripen on the Tree to be Extremely Good, after it is Grown Properly by "The LUSCIOUS All-Mineral Organic Method of Gardening!" Book 021B, which Means that the Topsoil must have all of the Proper Minerals in it. Remember the Grapes of Eschol, which the Children of Israel brought back from the Promised Land in *the Book of Joshua,* which Required 2 Strong Men to Carry just one Cluster! See the Fascinating Photos in: "Orgimmick Gardening at its Best!" (HOW to Grow Delicious Satisfying Foods without a 10 Million-Dollar Investment!) By The Worldwide People's Revolution!® Book 079, which is a Companion Book of: "Profitable Swanky MULCHING ROCKS!" (30 Advantages for Using Swanky Mulching Rocks in an All-Mineral Organic Garden!) By The Worldwide People's Revolution!® Book 098. They are Things that you have never Heard of!}

[_] 40-026 — "God Speaks and the Whole World Listens!" (Fire on the Mountain from the Burning Bush by the Spirit of Truths!) By The Worldwide People's Revolution!® Book 026B. {This Powerful Book contains the Best Noah Story of all of the Books, including that of Gilgamesh the Great of Ancient Babylon! God Personally Answers People's Important Questions. Therefore, do not Judge it, until you Study it, Carefully, with a Capital C: beCause, it is one of the Best Books in the Whole World, which is a Companion Book of: "LIGHTNING STRIKES Versus Lightning Bugs!" (HOW you can Become Moderately RICH, without Telling any Lies nor Selling any Trash!) By The Worldwide People's Revolution!® Book 074. But, Baal Worshipers will not Like it.}

15

[_] 40-027 — "Does a Good Soldier have to be a MURDERER?" (Seven Great Swanky Armies of Voluntary Working Soldiers!) By The Worldwide People's Revolution!® Book 027B. Chapter 03 contains a True-Life Story about a Dog Pile, which happened to the Author when he was just 10 Years Old, which nearly Killed him! However, being a Strong Healthy Farm Boy, he Survived it, and Lived to Tell the Most-Amazing Stories ever Written! See: "An Amazing Collection of Wit and Wisdom!" (The Marvelous Tale of the Colorful Peacock from Angel Ridge, and the Strong Rope of Everlasting Hope!) By The Worldwide People's Revolution!® Book 048. Just Check, **"The KO$T of a DIPSTIK!"** for which the Prosecuting Attorney sed, "I do not see how anything could be written that is Better than that. It should be in the Holy Bible!"

30

31

[_] 40-028 — "Thu Nq MAGNUFIID Verzhun uv Thu PROVERBZ uv KING SOLUMUN in Plaan Ingglish!" (The Understandable Version of the Famous Proverbs of King Solomon in Plain English!) By The Worldwide People's Revolution!® Book 028. {This Marvelous Book MAGNIFIES each and every Proverb of King Solomon, unto the Glory of the Great God of Inspiration, which is taken from the Original 4,000-page Book, which was written in less than 2 Months by the GIFT of Inspiration, which also contains the Famous Proverbs of Queen Izubelu, unto her 7 Dawterz! Just take your Sweet Time to Study it: beCause, it is a Genuine Collector's Item! See also: "The New MAGNIFIED Version of the HOLY KORAN!" (WHY MuhamMAD went to Hell for Spiritual MURDER!) By The Worldwide People's Revolution!® Book 089. Selah!}

15

[_] 40-029 — "Unlimited Enerjee 99 Percent Pollutions Free!" (HOW to Obtain FREE ElecTrickery, Worldwide!) By The Worldwide People's Revolution!® Book 029. {This Book contains the Jackson Brower Suicide, among many other Fascinating Subjects. The Updated Version is called: "UNLIMITED ENERGY 99 Percent Pollution-Free!" (HOW to Obtain Free ElecTrickery, Worldwide!) By The Worldwide People's Revolution!® Book 029B. They are NOT Identical Twin Books; but, either one is well Worth your Precious Time to Study it; and Reeding both Books will EXPAND your Mind considerably: beCause, that is the Nature of Inspired Books, which Require TIME to Soak into the Belly of your Mind, after you have Chewed on the Inspired Words, Carefully, like a Cow who Chews on her Cud 40 Times before Swallowing it! *Selah* Means to *STOP and THINK*. So, did you take the Time to Think?}

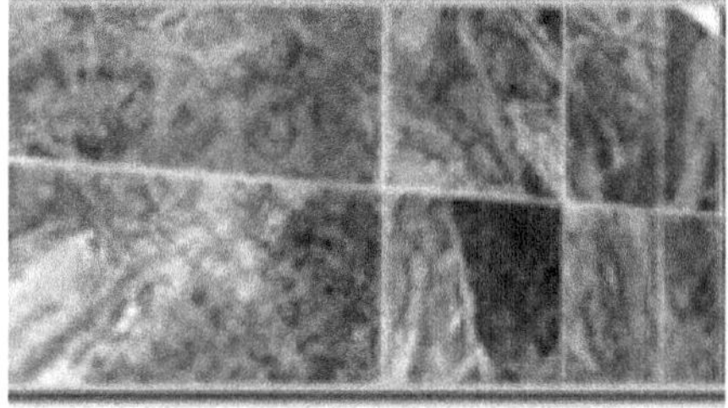

30

[_] 40-030 — **"FREEDUM uv SPEECH!" (U Speshoul Maguzeen uv Onist Upinyunz!) By The Worldwide People's Revolution!®** Book 030-0001, which contains the Great Advantages for Using Swanky Mulching Rocks in an All-Mineral Organic Garden, plus Baptism by Fire and Speaking in Foreign Languages! It is a Must-Read Book. The Cover Photo shows a Portion of the Author's Marbleous Indian Countertop, or Food Bar, which is just one Example of what you can also have in your own "Beautiful Swanky PALACES!" if you have the Honesty, Faith, Hope, Trust, Love, Patience, Persistence, Cooperation and OBEDIENCE that are Required for True Prosperity: beCause those are "The Seven Basic Spiritual Building Blocks of LIFE!" Book 036! Therefore, Ejukaat yourself, and you will be Glad that you did!

[_] 40-031 — "A Sure Cure for GUN VIOLENCE!" (HOW TO STOP GANG WARS and CRIMINAL SHOOTINGS!) By The Worldwide People's Revolution!® Book 031. {The Cover Photo shows a Picture of a Short Shotgun, which is Fully Loaded with Double 00 Shells, and is Ready for any Tax Master who might Attempt to Steal the Retirement Home, who never moved a Finger to Help Build the Rock Houses, whereby we moved more than 66,666,666 Pounds, by Hand, whose Property was Cunningly Stolen by that False Anti-Christ WICKED Cover-up Government, which allowed Bankers to Rob us of 30 Years of Hard Labor and more than 300,000 dollars-worth of Investments in our Uncommon American Farm, which is Explained in: "LIGHTNING STRIKES Versus Lightning Bugs!" (HOW you can Become Moderately RICH, without Telling any Lies nor Selling any Trash!) By The Worldwide People's Revolution!® Book 074, which contains many Photographs with Profound Explanations! Do not be left out in the Darkness of Ignorance. Get Informed, now: beCause, "The Great False Economy is now DEBUNKED!" Book 053.}

[_] 40-032 — "AIIRMWVC and Reasonable Solutions!" (Aliens, Illegal Immigrants, Refugees, Migrant Workers and other Victims of Capitalism!) By The Worldwide People's Revolution!® Book 032. {This Inspired Book contains *the New MAGNIFIED Version of Jobe 33,* which is very Enlightening! Tens of Millions of Victims of Capitalism, Communism, Socialism and War Games, are now Poor Miserable Displaced Refugees in Foreign Lands, who can now go back Home, and Help one another to Build their own "Beautiful Swanky PALACES!" (A New Concept in Living Habits — Swanky Palaces for Poor People!) By The Worldwide People's Revolution!® Book 066. Indeed, they only Need to DEMAND: "The GREAT Worldwide TELEVISED Court HEARING!" (That Great Meeting of the Most-Intelligent and Well-Educated Minds!) By The Worldwide People's Revolution!® Book 041B. So, will you Help them? Will you Do your Small but Meaningful Part to Spread this Good News? "The World from THEIR Point of View!" (WHO will Speak for the Masses of People, who have no Voice in Government?) By The Worldwide People's Revolution!® Book 140, can be Obtained for only 5 Dollars and 50 Cents, which will Speak FOR YOU, whereby you may Keep SILENT! Selah. Just Find a Poor Victim of Capitalism to Offer the Book to, and let it Speak for itself, O Friend of the Humble Honest Man from Galilee. See: "Reading it is Believing it!" (WHY I am the Healthy Happy International HERO of ALL Poor People!) By The Worldwide People's Revolution!® Book 132, "HOW to Conquer the World by Constructing GLORIOUS HOTELS!" (A Peaceful Takeover of the Evil Empires!) By The Worldwide People's Revolution!® Book 136, plus: "The Affordable Constitutional Health Care Act!" (A New Amendment to the Constitution for the United States of North America!) By The Worldwide People's Revolution!® Book 137, plus: "I did NOT Vote!" (There are 7 Billion Reasons!) By The Worldwide People's Revolution!® Book 138, plus: "Would you Vote for Jesus Christ to be your Elected King?" (The Skeptic will say that Jesus Christ would never be Campaigning for any Election Deceptions!) By The Worldwide People's Revolution!® Book 139.}

[_] 40-033 — "MARK TWAIN Races for the PRESIDENCY with a Landslide VICTORY!" (The 2020 Presidential Candidates Desperately Need Some STRONG Undefeatable COMPETITION!) By The Worldwide People's Revolution!® Book 033B. {This Book contains a Part of the Author's Autobiography, and his Personal Answers to the Questions in: "The Complete SURVEYS of our VALUES!" (SURVEYS of Religious Spiritual Political Governmental Sexual Social Moral Economic Business Labor Habitual and Miscellaneous VALUES!) By The Worldwide Peoples Revolution!® Book 059. **The CONDENSED Version** is Book 033C, which most People Prefer: beCause, it gets right to the Point, without Beating around any Bushes, as they say.}

1

You can easily Recognize the 2 Different Books by the Colors of their Subtitles, and the Words at the Top of the Front Cover. Do not allow Amazon to Fool you by their own Deceptions. There are several Different Editions of each Book. For some Unknown Reason, Amazon does not like to Sell the 8.5 by 11-inch Colored Editions, which are the least Expensive and the Best Books, in large easy-to-read Print. The E-Books are the Cheapest, and do not make Good Collector's Items: beCause they are only Electronic. The 6 by 9 Colored Editions are the most Expensive, and do not have Line Numbers for easy References; and the Screen Shots and Pictures are normally smaller and more Difficult to read. We much Prefer the large Colored Editions, which make a Beautiful Book Display under Glass on any Wall in any House. Even the Queen of England agrees with that, and she Livz in a Palace; but, NOT in a Swanky Palace! ‡

16
17
18

[ ] 40-034 — "ECCLESIASTES Uncovered and Recovered!" (The New MAGNIFIED Version of Ecclesiastes and the Song of Solomon in Plain English!) By The Worldwide People's Revolution!® Book 034. {This is the Book that contains the Famous Sayings for *"There is a Time to be Born, and a Time to Die …"* which has been Greatly MAGNIFIED for your Enlightenment. It makes a Nice Gift for anyone who Likes to Read. Most People do not: beCause, "The Public School of IGNERUNT FQLZ!" (HOW we have been GRAATLEE DISEEVD by Capitalism!) By The Worldwide People's Revolution!® Book 024B, has "Turned them Off," as they say, whereby they do not Want to read another Book. Indeed, what "they" Want is X-number of Work Slaves, Tax Slaves, Insurance Slaves, Interest Slaves, Mortgage Slaves, Transportation Slaves, ElecTrickery Bills Slaves, Gas Bills Slaves, Food Bills Slaves, Water Bills Slaves, Telephone Bills Slaves, Internet Bills Slaves, Entertainment Bills Slaves, Drug Bills Slaves, Doctor Bills Slaves, Hospital Bills Slaves, Childcare Bills Slaves, etc.}

[ ] 40-035 — "The Environmentalists' Perfect Paradise!" (HOW almost Everyone can be Living in a Beautiful Manmade Paradise!) By The Worldwide People's Revolution!® Book 035C. {This Book contains the NMV of *Psalm 48,* which will Amaze you, O Lady Doubtfulness! It is a Companion Book of: "The Secret City of the Great King!" (HOW the True Church will Escape from the Great Tribulation!) By The Worldwide People's Revolution!® Book 042. Of course, you can Mock it, along with a lot of other Provable Truths; but, only you will Lose Out. After all, our Selected King has Seen that Holy City, himself! ‡ Therefore, he Knows for a Fact that it is for REAL; but, you do not have to Believe it, nor Find yourself Living within it; but, Jesus went to Prepare a Place for those who Believe Provable Truths! Therefore, why be just another Ignorant Fool? Why not Discover what is Required? Selah.}

1

16

[_] 40-036 — "The Seven Basic Spiritual Building Blocks of LIFE!" (Faith Hope Trust Love Patience Persistence and Obedience!) By The Worldwide People's Revolution!® Book 036. {This Book contains the Mockingbird's Version of *Hebrews 11,* plus the NMV of *First Corinthians 13,* among many other "Goodies." Remember that the Greatest Truths must be Hidden from the Mockingbirds and Ignorant Fools: beCause, they are not Worthy of any Positions within the Holy Kingdom of All that is GOOD. Therefore, God will Blind them from Seeing the Way Out of Sodom and Gomorrah, and even Transform them into "Pillars of Salt," if they Look Back with Longing Desires on their Past Sins. Therefore, it is Better for their Souls to Deny themselves of any and all such Vain Pleasures: beCause, the Eyes of Unbelievers have never Seen the Glorious Things that God has Prepared for those who Love him.}

31

32

[_] 40-037 — "DIETS!" (A Reasonable Solution for the "Eternal Controversy"!) By The Worldwide People's Revolution!® Book 037. {There are thousands, and perhaps tens of thousands of Diet Plans for Mankind; but, *"only one Good Thing is Needed,"* as Jesus told Martha, as she was Complaining about Mary not Helping her to Fix the Meal; and that one Thing is Revealed within this Inspired Book for whomever has the Faith to Study it. For those who Lack the Necessary Money, they should read: "HOW to Conquer the World by Constructing GLORIOUS HOTELS!" (A Peaceful Takeover of the Evil Empires!) **By** The Worldwide People's Revolution!® Book 136. The Answer might be Found in the Free Book Preview. †§‡}

[_] 40-038 — "The Nature of CAPITALISM!" (A List of the EVILS of CAPITALISM!) By The Worldwide People's Revolution!® Book 038. {Most People do not Stop to Think about any of the Evils of Capitalism: beCause, they must Obtain Money, just to Stay Alive in such an Evil Empire; but, the True Christian Plan is Revealed in: "The New MAGNIFIED Version of the Book of ACTS!" (The Understandable Version of the Acts of the Apostles in Plain English!) By The Worldwide People's Revolution!® Book 063, which is Designed for Mockingbirds to Mock: beCause, they do not Deserve the True Riches, nor even a Good Meal at one of those "Royal Swanky Buffets!" (The Best Feasts in the Whole World!) By The Worldwide People's Revolution!® Book 103. Do not Feel Sorry for them; but, Feel Sorry for yourself, O Painted Skunk! ‡}

[_] 40-039 — "SWANGKEENOMIKS Rules the Roost!" (HOW all People can Prosper in a RIIT WAA, and STOP Polluting the Earth with Capitalist TRASH!) By The Worldwide People's Revolution!® Book 039. {The Cover Photo shows a Portion of the Author's Retirement Home, before the 5,000+ square-feet Concrete Roof was Installed, after moving more than 66 Million Pounds by Hand, and mostly by his own Boastful Hands! You can possibly Discover the Cover Photo on the Inside of this Book; but, if not, just keep Searching in those Free Book Previews: beCause, you can Discover a LOT of Important Information within those Previews, if you just have the Faith to LOOK! But, of course, you will also have to have the Faith to ACT on what you Learn, before it becomes Meaningful.}

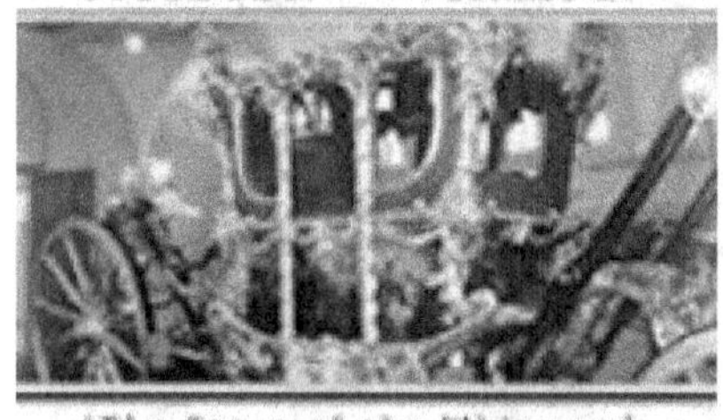

[_] 40-040 — "The New MAGNIFIED Version of The Book of MORMON!" (The Story of the White and Dark Indians in the Americas!) By Big Chief Stands Over Bull in the River of Life with a Mile-High Erectile Dysfunction! Book 040, which comes in 2 Volumes of about 500 Pages, each. The Cover Photo on the First Volume shows the Queen of England's Golden Coach, and the Cover Photo on the Second Volume shows a Small Portion of one of many Polished Spanish Marble Walls in our Selected King's Retirement Home, which is worth a thousand dollars per square yard, which is another Example of what you can also have, if you simply OBEY your Righteous KING, who is otherwise known as a Peabrain PEACOCK and Grade School DROPOUT! All such Marble is very Inspiring. No one could Study it for very long without Believing in a Great Creator God. The Picture does not do it Justice. You would have to See it in Person, and Wash it with Pure Water to bring Out the Beauty of it. You can See Close-up Views of it in other Books. Theses Books do not have Internal Photographs of anything. Selah.

15

30
31

45
46

[_] 40-041 — "The GREAT Worldwide TELEVISED Court HEARING!" (That Great Meeting of the Most-Intelligent and Well-Educated Minds!) **By The Worldwide People's Revolution!**® Book 041B. {This is the Book that the World has long been Waiting for: beCause it will Overthrow the Evil Empires, and make it Possible to Establish **"The New RIGHTEOUS One-World Government!" (HOW to Establish a Righteous One-World Government without Going to WAR!) By The Worldwide People's Revolution!**® Book 056. This is the Greatest Idea since the Invention of the Light Bulb, Guaranteed! Therefore, please Study it and tell your Friends and Naaberz about it: beCause, it could Save your Soul and their Souls from a LOT of Needless Suffering. Selah! †§‡}

[_] 40-042 — **"The Secret City of the Great King!" (HOW the True Church will Escape from the Great Tribulation!) By The Worldwide People's Revolution!**® Book 042. {Be Sure to Inform your Friends, Relatives and Naaberz about this Wonderful Book: beCause they might also Want to Escape! Once again, it is a Highly-Camouflaged Book, which is Deliberately Designed by God to Deter the Liars, Hypocrites, Mockers, and Scoffers. May they all go through the Great Tribulation, just for their Unbelief in Provable Truths, whereby their Minds and Hearts might be Refined and Purified: beCause, there is no other Way that they can be Saved from all of their Sins, and especially from their Dietary Sins, which are their Greatest Sins; but, they are Unaware of it: beCause the Irreverent LOUDMOUTH Windbag Hole-in-his-Head never Told them! In Fact, he is also Unaware of any such Dietary Sins, himself! †§‡}

[_] 40-043 — **"Terrorists Beware that your Days are Numbered!" (HOW to Bring those Terrorist Attacks to a Screeching HALT!) By The Worldwide People's Revolution!**® Book 043. {This Book also contains the Fascinating *Book of LEHI,* which was Lost in the Darkness of Ignorance; but, it has now been Restored in its Original Format, including all Capitalized Words, which have Double and even Triple Meanings! For Example, George Warmonger Bush is still running Loose in the Concrete Jungle with Little Dick Chicanery, who Vainly Imagined that they got by with their Attack on Iraq for the Sins of **"Conspiracy Theories did it!" (The Evil Events of September 11th 2001 are Revisited by a Wise Son of King Solomon!) By The Worldwide People's Revolution!**® Book 128. You are Welcome to Believe whatever Lies that you Like; but, during God's Judgment Day, nothing will be Top Secret, nor Hidden.} †‡

15

31 †§‡
32

[_] 40-044 — "The New MAGNIFIED Version of ISAIAH in Plain English!" (The Understandable Version of the Book of Isaiah!) By The Worldwide People's Revolution!® Book 044. {The Cover Photo shows a Swanky Potato and Avocado Salad with Sweet Peas and Corn, among other "Secret" Ingredients, which are Revealed within the Book. Remember that you can read many Words for Free in the Book Previews on www.Amazon.com.usa or UK. The EU and United Kingdom seem to have their Act more "Together" than Spain, France, and other "Foreign Languages," which are not Foreign to them; but, to US. For Example, they do not know that the United States is Abbreviated as U.S.A., or U.S., and not us, even if they Look similar to a Robot Computer Reader, which seems to not be Able to Distinguish the Difference. Maybe they will Fix it in 10000?}

[_] 40-045 — "HOW to Become a HOLY Man!" (40 Good Reasons WHY People Should FAST and PRAY!) By The Worldwide People's Revolution!® Book 045, which is a Companion Book of the next Book. Here is a Picture of a Holy Man in Body, if not in Mind nor Spirit. Just Hope that you do Better than he did, before you Criticize him. He is only 154 Years Old, and still Looking Good! Of course, you should not Believe it; but, it would not Damage your Soul by one Degree, even if you did Believe it. Indeed, you probably Believe *the Book of Genesis,* which has many Exaggerations and Lies; but, none of them will Send you to Hell so Quickly as False Christian Doctrines — such as, "There is no Need for Fasting: beCause, we are Saved by Faith, alone!" Tell that to the Holy Man, who Walked on the Water, whose Disciples are still Walking on the Water, defying Gravity, and Magnifying God.

33

15

[_] 40-046 — "The Proper RULES for FASTING!" (The Complete Instruction Manual for True Repentance!) By The Worldwide People's Revolution!® Book 046, which is a Companion Book of the above-mentioned Book, which contains a True-Life Story about an Old Black Mare called Lucy, who Fasted for 30 Days without Consuming Food nor Water, who was Physiologically "Born Again," as Jesus might say. See the Full Details in: "The New MAGNIFIED Version of The GOOD NEWS According to Saint JOHN!" (The Gospel According to Saint John Zebedee Boanerges in Plain English!) By The Worldwide People's Revolution!® Book 062, which contains many Inspiring Photographs with Enlightening Explanations! Have some Faith, O Lady Doubtfulness, and BELIEVE Truths!

29

[_] 40-047 — "Are Americans the Most-STUPID People who ever Lived?" (HOW Working People can PROSPER and Live in PEACE Under the Rulership of a RIGHTEOUS KING!) By The Worldwide People's Revolution!® Book 047. {The Cover Photo shows a large Portion of the Author's Living Room Floor, which is worth 100,000$, which is just another Good Example of what you can also have, just for Loving and Obeying your Selected King, who is not Asking you to Say nor Do any Evil Things! Indeed, he is even Proposing to do Away with ALL Taxes, and Liberate all of the Capitalist, Socialist and Communist Slaves. Do you have something Against that, O Church Mice? If so, Send your Message to the E-mail Address on the Back Cover.}

44

[_] 40-048 — "An Amazing Collection of Wit and Wisdom!" (The Marvelous Tale of the Colorful Peacock from Angel Ridge, and the Strong Rope of Everlasting Hope!) By The Worldwide People's Revolution!® Book 048. {The Cover Photo shows a Colorful Peacock Book Display, you might say, which will be Greatly Enhanced during the Future, when all 364+ Inspired Books are on Display in a Beautiful Swanky Truth-brary, as Opposed to the Public LIE-brary, which has nothing to Compare with the Amazing Tale Feathers of the Colorful Peacock from Angel Ridge, at King's Mountain, Kentucky 40442 U.S.A., who Wrote all of these 140 Inspired Books in less than 6 Years! Moreover, we Challenge you to Do any Better, O Colorful Roosters, White Ducks, and Squawking Crows. Just Stretch Out your Wings of Great Faith, and Present your own Magnificent Plan for Worldwide Law, Order,

45 Obedience, Peace and True Prosperity, whereby we might Study it, and put a Crown on your Hed.}

15

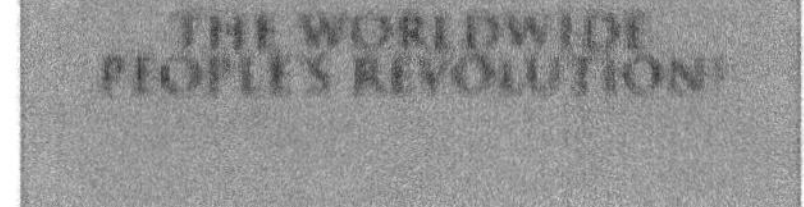

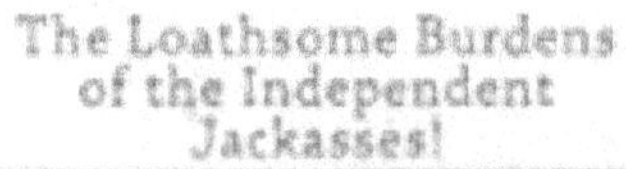

[_] 40-049 — "Justifications for Capitalizations!" (WHY our Selected King DEFIES the School of FOOLS by Capitalizing LOVE and HATE!) By The Worldwide People's Revolution!® Book 049. {Most Americans would not put a Capital B on Bite, even if some Algaegators took Big Bites Out of their own Rumps: beCause, it is not their Tradition to Capitalize Love, which would not be Doing any such Mean Things. However, when the Rains Stop, and their Bellybuttons are Rubbing on their Backbones for Hunger and Thirst, they will probably Think about Capitalizing Water, Climate Changes, Pollution, and "The New RIGHTEOUS One-World Government!" (HOW to Establish a Righteous One-World Government without Going to WAR!) By The Worldwide People's Revolution!® Book 056, since that alone can Fix it! ‡}

[_] 40-050 — "The END of CONFUSION!" (The Great CELEBRATION of the Magnificent Wedding of the Most-Humble, Honest Nations, and the Grand Year of JUBILEE!) By The Worldwide People's Revolution!® Book 050. {Just Try to Visualize those **"Seven Great Armies of Voluntary Working Soldiers,"** Marching through the Valley of Megiddo, being Dressed in their Colorful Robes, while the Band Plays *The Battle Hymn of the Republic,* and the Choirs Sing the Praises of the Great KING of Kings! What a Sight and Sound that will be, which will be Climaxed in "The Great World TEMPLE of PEACE," when the Nations will get Married, along with our Elected King! Come one, come all to "The GREAT Worldwide TELEVISED Court HEARING," by Means of your Wide Flat-screen TVs, whereby you might Learn Why, When and How!‡}

[_] 40-051 — "The Loathsome Burdens of the Independent Jackasses!" (A New Civilized Approach for Quietly Solving our Massive Problems!) By The Worldwide People's Revolution!® Book 051. {Just Think about the Multitude of almost Worthless Meetings of the Minds, who Strained themselves to Think of Reasonable Solutions for our Massive Problems, who sometimes even Prayed to God for Help; but, the Best Solutions have been here for no less than 40 Years — Thanks to the Spirit of Inspiration from GOD, who Revealed "Guaranteed Solutions!" (HOW to Solve our Local and Global Problems in the Most-Rational Manner Possible!) By The Worldwide People's Revolution!® Book 080, to our Selected King, who has Zero Challengers! See: "Provable Truths that True Christians cannot Rightly Deny!" (A Fair Challenge for all Professing "Christians" to Meditate on with Honest Open Minds!) By The Worldwide People's Revolution!® B-086. No Government Official has anything Comparable.}

15

16

[_] 40-052 — "Are we Tax Slaves of a Lower Order than those Lying Conniving EDOMITES!" (HOW to be Liberated From all Forms of Slavery, Worldwide!) By The Worldwide People's Revolution!® Book 052B. {This Inspired Book once had another Title and Author, which was not Acceptable by Amazon, which has now been Restored in all of its Naked Glory, and is Published by more Trustworthy People, who are not Afraid of Controversies, nor of: "The Swanky Sword of Divine Truths!" (The Most-Powerful Weapon in the Whole Universe!) By The Worldwide People's Revolution!® Book 067. The Popularity of any Inspired Book among Ignorant Fools is no Good Criteria for Condemning it: beCause, the Masses of People often Change their Minds. They even Tried to Burn the Bible, during the Dark Ages, when most People never red it. †§‡}

[_] 40-053 — "The Great False Economy is now DEBUNKED!" (Adolf Hitler had a much Better Economic System!) By The Worldwide People's Revolution!® Book 053. {Trust me, Adolf was no Saint; but, during the Day of God's Judgment, he will be Justified, while his Anti-Christ Opponents will be Condemned: beCause they Refused to Attend a Worldwide Radio Debate with Adolf Hitler, whose Arguments will Stand Up during the Day of Judgment, which would have Prevented World War 2, and thus Saved the Lives of no less than 60 Million People! Likewise, we Tax Slaves must now Act more Wisely, and Demand "The GREAT Worldwide TELEVISED Court HEARING," Book 041B, whereby we might Save the World from that Dreadful Battle of Megiddo, often called *Armageddon!* Yes, the Ball is now in YOUR Hands, O Potential Friend or Enemy, and you are now Responsible for it. Therefore, do not Shirk your Duty as a Free Citizen; but, Help us to Spread this Message, far and wide, whereby the Masses of People will be Demanding The GWTCH, and thus, Prevent "The Great ATOMIC NIGHTMARE!" (The Saddest Story in World History!) By The Great White Bald Eagle! Book 099. See: "HOW to Conquer the World by Constructing GLORIOUS HOTELS!" (A Peaceful Takeover of the Evil Empires!) **By** The Worldwide People's Revolution!® Book 136. It is really quite Simple, if you have the Faith to Visualize it. Most People do NOT: beCause, they Refuse to even Think about it, let alone, Meditate on it, both Day and Night, until they See the Need for it. But, once you Learn the Truth about Swanky Fortresses, all of your Thots will Forever Circulate around to that same Starting Point: beCause of the 5,000-plus Advantages for Building them and Living within the Secure Borders of them! Therefore, do not Attempt to Block those Fortresses Out of your Mind: beCause, that will only Darken your Good Understanding, and even Blind your Spiritual Mind to them, whereby you will end up Speaking Evil of that which is GOOD, which is a Major Sin, O Modern Pharisee. Therefore, just Humble yourself and Accept all Provable Truths: beCause, that can Save you from a LOT of Em-bare-assment, as Honest "Nigger Jim" might say to Huck Finn, who also Knows that it is the Truth, even if he does not Know all of the Fine Details about it, as Tom Sawyer and Juj Thatcher might.}

[_] 40-054 — "The UGLY Scarred Dishonest Face of Poor Old Miserable UNCLE SAM!" (A Memorial Day Legacy!) By The Worldwide People's Revolution!® Book 054. {NOTE: This Inspired Book was also Suppressed by Amazon, who will be most Ashamed of themselves if they do not Un-suppress it during the Future: beCause it will also be Published by People of Greater Faith, who Know for a Fact that it is the TRUTH! Therefore, just be Patient. Search for Book 054B, *King James Version.* *"Seek, and you shall Find, Knock on the Door with Faith, and it will be Opened; Give Truths, and they will be Given to you — Pressed Down, Shaken Together, and Running Over shall Men Give Precious Gemstones of Provable Truths into your Bosom." — NMV.* Any given Truth could Save you thousands of Dollars, if not Millions! I have Proof of it! ‡}

[_] 40-055 — "The United States of the Whole World!" (A True Global Economy for the Masses of Working People!) By The Worldwide People's Revolution!® Book 055. {This Inspired Book contains many Colored Photographs with Explanations. It is a Good Book to Publish in Foreign Nations, who are not so Blinded by their Pride, who can See the Mountain of Lies much Better at a Distance from them: beCause of not being a Part of the American Corruption, which is like Standing in the Middle of a HUGE Capitalist Trash Dump with Broken Field Glasses, covered with Mud on the Lenses. Just the STINK should be enough to Warn you about its Evilness. Therefore, sit down in your Comfortable Rocking Chair, and Read another Good Book: beCause, there will be something to Inspire you. Just the Pictures will Inspire you a whole lot, O Reader, if you Study them, Carefully and Prayerfully.} †‡

[_] 40-056 — "The New RIGHTEOUS One-World Government!" (HOW to Establish a Righteous One-World Government without Going to WAR!) By The Worldwide People's Revolution!® Book 056. {This is a KEY Book, which everyone should Study Carefully and Prayerfully. This is a Companion Book of **"The New RIGHTEOUS One-World Government UPDATED!"** Book 056B, which also has a lot of Pictures to Study; but, the Original Book contains Important Information that cannot be Found in the Updated Version. We Recommend that everyone should Study ALL of the Inspired Books in their Swanky Truth-braries. Mark the Statements that you Agree with, using a DARK GREEN-X Mark in the Box. But, if you Disagree, use a LARGE RED-X Mark in the Box.}

45

It is a Totally New Book, and Exceptionally Good.

15

[_] 40-057 — "Those Ridiculous Contradictions within the Holy Bible!" (HOW to Read the so-Called Bible with an Honest Open Mind!) By The Worldwide People's Revolution!® Book 057. {NOTE: Many Professing "Christians" Falsely Claim that their so-called *"Holy Bibles"* do not Contain any Contradictions, being "the Infallible Inspired Word of the Living God," but, without the Capitalized Words, and without Explaining just WHY there are more than 200 Contradictory Versions of it! This Book Reveals how to Deal with those Biblical Problems, and come to Understand WHY God Allowed it to Happen for the Truth's Sake, which is Explained in Chapter 08 of "The Affordable Constitutional Health Care Act!" (A New Amendment to the Constitution for the United States of North America!) **By** The Worldwide

30 People's Revolution!® Book 137. Trust God: beCause, you have never Heard that Explanation
31 before now. See also: "C-SPAN-DEX!" (Your Filtered View of Bad Government!) By The
32 Worldwide People's Revolution!® Book 097.}
33

[_] 40-058 — "The Divided States of United Lies!" (The so-called "United States of North America" in Disguise!) By The Worldwide People's Revolution!® Book 058. {NOTE: This is perhaps the most Referred to Book among all of the Books by our Selected King; but, that does not Mean that it is his Best Book by any Means, which is Well Camouflaged: so that it will Survive the Test of Time, even if the others are BURNED by the Anti-Christ Followers of Satan, who are Possession Worshipers of the Worst Kind, who Seek to Justify American Lies, rather than Quickly Confess them, and thus Escape from their Self-made Prison of Propagandish Lies! Just be Perfectly Honest, and you will have no Problem with any of our Selected King's Inspired Literature.}

[_] 40-059 — "The Complete SURVEYS of our VALUES!" (SURVEYS of Religious Spiritual Political Governmental Sexual Social Moral Economical Business Labor Habitual and Miscellaneous VALUES!) By The Worldwide People's Revolution!® Book 059. {NOTE: According to our Selected King, every Potential Leader in the Whole World should Fill Out and File those Surveys on the Internet for everyone to Study, whereby the Best People might be Elected by those Wise People, who have also Filled Out the Simplistic Surveys of their own Values, whereby they will be Qualified to VOTE. Otherwise, they will not be Qualified to Vote, which will Eliminate a LOT of Wasted Money on Election Deceptions, while at the same Time it will Educate a lot of Ignorant People, who Desperately Need to Study that Inspired Book before Voting for another Dimwitcrat, Reprobate, or Crazy Jackass!}

[_] 40-059B — "The Simplistic SURVEYS of our VALUES!" Book 059B. (The Cover Photo shows some Beautiful African Antelopes, who are Free with a Capital F.) If you can Discover the Correct Free Book Previews on Amazon, you can fill up your Heart on those Words, alone. This is one such Book, which comes in 5 Editions. We suggest that you Reed all 5 Free Book Previews.

[_] 40-060 — "HOW to Get our PRIORITIES in ORDER!" (The Glories of Democracy; and, Does DEMON-ocracy have its Priorities in Order?) By The Worldwide People's Revolution!® Book 060. This Book will need to be Re-written by a Collective Group of Wise People, who will Contribute their True-Life Stories during the Future, when they Wake Up and come to their Right Senses with the Prodigal Son of *Luke 15*. See the next Book, 061. This is a Companion Book of: "The Peabrain Peacock Studies Demon-ocracy!" (A Guaranteed Soution for the Plastic Trash Problem!) **By** The Worldwide People's Revolution!® Book 141. Most People have no Idea HOW to go about getting their Priorities in Order. What should they Do First — read the Bible, go to School, Hatch Eggs, or what? They are Completely LOST on that Subject, and so are we.

15

29

30

45

[_] 40-061 — "The New MAGNIFIED Version of The GOOD NEWS According to Saint LUKE!" (The Magnified Gospel of Saint Luke in Plain English!) By The Worldwide People's Revolution!® Book 061, which is by Far the Best Version of that Gospel on the Earth, which has no Rivals at all among the other 200+ Versions. Guaranteed! Just read *the Prodigal Son* in *Luke 15,* and you will See what we Mean. It is many Times Better than any other Version. It is Tempting to Quote it, right here, on this Page; but, you can find it and all of the other Parables in the Gospel of Saint Luke. It is Masterful Literature at its Best! Try the Parable of the Rich Man and Lazarus, if you Think that the Fake Trumpeter will find any Position in the Kingdom of God. Not even Prancing Nancy will come Close to Entering it. †§‡§§

[_] 40-062 — "The New MAGNIFIED Version of The GOOD NEWS According to Saint JOHN!" (The Gospel According to Saint John Zebedee Boanerges [pronounced Boo-an-er-jeez] in Plain English!) By The Worldwide People's Revolution!® Book 062, which also has no Rivals among all of the other Versions: beCause this is no Translation of anything; but, it is the Inspired Words of the Living God, which were Revealed by the Holy Spirit to our Selected King, who has not Died, yet. This is perhaps the most Graceful and Flowing Book of the entire Holy Bible, which is what one would Expect from the Holy Spirit. No other Version comes even Close to Comparing with it for Fine Well-crafted Words of Provable Truths. It makes you Happy, just to Reed it. It is a Marvelous Book for 12-year-old Boys to Reed. Girls should be at least 18.

[_] 40-063 — "The New MAGNIFIED Version of the Book of ACTS!" (The Understandable Version of the Acts of the Apostles in Plain English!) By The Worldwide People's Revolution!® Book 063. {This Inspired Book makes it Understandable WHY the Jews Hated the Apostles so much. You will have to Read it to Believe it, which makes Perfect Sense. However, we must Warn you that there is Adult Contents within this Inspired Book, which might be Misunderstood by Children, who are under 18 Years Old, even though, no one has Complained about it, so far. Nevertheless, we Expect that some People will Complain about it during the Future: beCause, it is about the Apostle Paul Circumcising Poor Little Timothy, after Winning an Argument against Saint Peter about not being Saved by the Works of the Law! And a Holy Angel Saves the Day! Smile.}

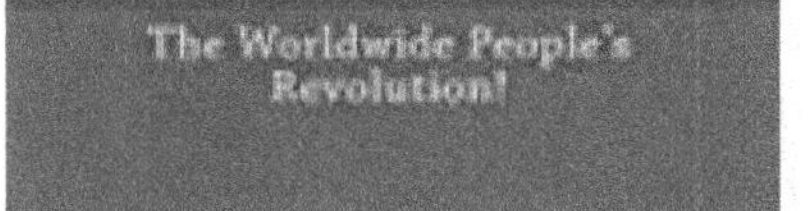

15

16

[_] 40-064 — "The New MAGNIFIED Version of the PSALMS of King David!" (The Understandable Version of the Famous Psalms in Plain English!) By The Worldwide People's Revolution!® Book 064. You will be Amazed! There is a HUGE Amount of True Nolij in the *Psalms,* which could be the Reason for it being the "Most-red Book" in the entire Bible. Actually, it is the Most-Comforting Book in the entire Bible, which is made Famous by *Psalm 24,* which this Inspired Book MAGNIFIES for Jesus Christ, himself: beCause, several Chapters were written just for him, including *Psalm 22 through 24,* specifically. Jesus also Quoted more Words from the *Psalms,* than from any other Book of the *Holy Bible.* It is a Shame that he never got to Reed the New MAGNIFIED Version of it, which he would have no doubt Loved the most. Almost everyone does. Repetitious Psalms have been Dropped from the Book. Sorry. §‡

31

32

[_] 40-065 — "A List of FAIR Swanky Wages!" (The Equitable Wage System!) By The Worldwide People's Revolution!® Book 065. {All Hardworking People will LOVE this Good Book! You will also, if you Study it Carefully: beCause, it Reveals how everyone can get FAIR Wages for the First Time in World History, whereby no one will have any Cause for Complaining about Low Wages, even if they are just Children, who can only Peel Carrots for making Fresh Carrot Juice: beCause, the Peelings are Bitter and perhaps Dirty. Therefore, after the Carrots are Washed with Clean Water, they should be Air-Dried and Peeled Properly, even if the Peeler is Slow and half Asleep. After all, it is a Job that can be done while Sitting in a Recliner, while Listening to the News on TV or Radio, which almost any Old Person can Do for 3 to 4 Hours per Day, and Earn a Living.}

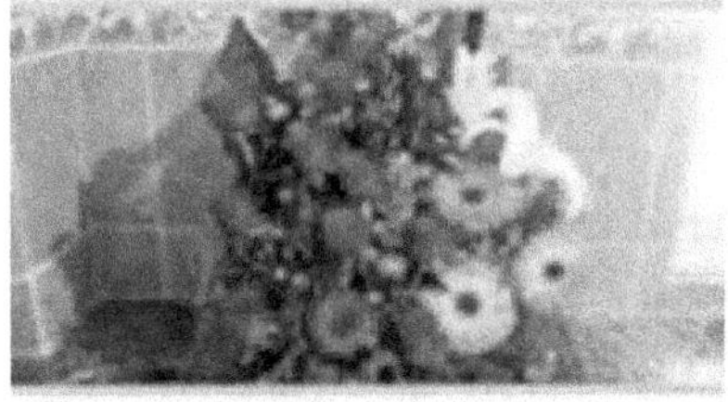

[_] 40-066 — "Beautiful Swanky PALACES!" (A New Concept in Living Habits — Swanky Palaces for Poor People!) By The Worldwide People's Revolution!® Book 066. {You have no Idea what a "Swanky Palace" IS, unless you have read this Unique Book, or another one that Describes those Palaces, and several Books do; but, this one has the Best Description, which you can reed in the Free Book Previews, if you reed all of them. However, the Book goes into Great Details to make it all Perfectly Clear for the Children to Understand. Most Old People will not be at all Interested in Swanky Palaces: beCause of being too Old and Tired to Enjoy them. Therefore, they should Commit themselves to those "Beautiful Swanky FASTING SANITARIUMS!" (HOW to Learn Good Self-Discipline!) **By The Worldwide People's Revolution!® Book 115. ENJOY!}**

[_] 40-067 — "The Swanky Sword of Divine Truths!" (The Most-Powerful Weapon in the Whole Universe!) By The Worldwide People's Revolution!® Book 067. {The very Reason that our Selected King has no Rivals is beCause of the Swanky Sword of Divine Truths, which no one can Defeat by any Means. Therefore, you Need to have it on your own Side, whereby no one can Defeat your Arguments! Be Strong, be Brave, have Faith and put on the Whole Armor of GOD! The Cover Photo is a little Weird: beCause, the Sword is Laying Down at the Bottom of the Photo. It got Cut Off by Miss Amazon Photo Lab. The Book is not Tall enough for the Photo to be Standing Upright. Sorry about that. People are Welcome to Mock the Robe, in spite of the Fact that Robes have more than 77 Advantages for Men. For Example, you cannot Forget to Zip Up your Pants. Sum Politicians do.}

[_] 40-068 — "Has your Life become Extremely Complicated?" (HOW to Live a SIMPLE Life!) By The Worldwide People's Revolution!® Book 068. {Many People are not even Aware of just how Complicated their Lives are, until suddenly they are ready to Commit Suicide; but, they are not Ready to Die and Meet their Maker, who is the Chief Juj. Or, is he? We are Told that "all men were created equal," in the Image of some God. But, were they? Not According to the *Holy Bible,* which makes it Clear in *Number 16,* which goes into Great Details about it. It is Best to Prevent all such Evil Things; and this Book tells HOW to Simplify our Lives by Living within those "GLORIOUS Swanky Hotels Castles and Fortresses!" (Beautiful Planned City States for WISE Intelligent Well-Educated People with Common Sense and Good Understanding!) By The Worldwide People's Revolution!® Book 019B. You and everyone else will Love it, once you get Adjusted to it, O Flexible Believer.}

[_] 40-069 — "The IDEAL Place to Live!" (HOW to Discover the Ideal Place to Live!) By The Worldwide People's Revolution!® Book 069. {NOTE: Our Selected King Searched the World over, and did not Discover any Idea Place to Live. Therefore, he Concluded that we must Make our own. Yes, we must Build those "GLORIOUS Swanky Hotels Castles and Fortresses!" even if we must DRAFT "Seven Great Armies of Working Soldiers!" (HOW to Provide a Way for Everyone to WORK: so as to Eliminate Poverty, Crimes, Drug Abuses, Prisons and Unnecessary Taxes!) By The Worldwide People's Revolution!® Book 015B; and what on this Good Earth could Prove to be more Profitable than that, and without going to WAR, Selling any Capitalist Trash, nor Producing any Criminals? Try to Study it for a Year or 3, before you Hang yourself, O … †§‡}

14

28

42

[_] 40-070 — "Our Elected King Who Speaks Out!" (It is High Time for some Sane Person to Get Control of this Insane World!) By The Worldwide People's Revolution!® Book 070. {This Inspired Book contains a Special Speech that is Addressed to both Houses of the Congress in Washington. You will Love it, O Honest Man of Greater Faith! You might even find most of it in the Free Book Preview. If not, you can Blame Amazon, who seem to Lack Good Judgment. After all, it is a very Special Speech, and a Good Introduction to the Book. No Congressman ever gave a Better Speech, as far as we know. But, if you know of one, please let us know where to Find it. See the Back Cover of any Recent Book for the E-mail Address. ‡}

[_] 40-071 — "How GAY is GOD?" (Oh, the Wonders of it all, when it ALL Hangs Out!) By The Worldwide People's Revolution!® Book 071. {Do not Judge the Book, until you have Carefully "Red" all of it. You will be Surprised by the Provable Truths within it, and Greatly Humored by the Author's Exceptionally Good Humor, who is less Gay than God, who has never had any Sexual Intercourse during his entire Life! In other Words, he is a VIRGIN, if you can Believe it! Most People find that too Difficult to Believe; but, it is True. Please do not Ask us HOW it could be True; but, the *Holy Bible* does Mention such People. (See *Revelation 14:4, Gay King James Version.*) However, there are Overwhelming Evidences that God is GAY! Just Look at the Cover Photo for the Irrefutable Proof! †§‡§§}

[_] 40-072 — "LIGHTNING STRIKES Versus Lightning Bugs and Impotent Fireflies!" (A Memorial Photo Album of some Real American Heroes!) By The Worldwide People's Revolution!® Book 072. {NOTE: This Book is Unique among all of the Books by our Selected King: beCause he did not get to Proof-read it before the Computer Crashed. It just Happened to be Saved on a Computer Chip before the Computer Crashed, and therefore it was Saved in PDF. But, the Corrections did not get made, which makes it a Special Collector's Item, which has more than 100 Colored Photos, which was what Caused the Crash. So, what Appeared to be BAD, was Actually GOOD! God Knows that it all Turned Out to be Good, including that BIG Red Spot on Jupiter, which is Symbolical of the Eye of God!} ††‡

43

[_] 40-073 — "The BEST of CAPITALISM!" (Corrections for: "LIGHTNING STRIKES Versus Lightning Bugs and Impotent Fireflies!") Book 073. {It is a completely new Book, except for those Corrections; and it is one of the Best Books in the Whole World, which all Honest People will Love. However, like ALL of the Books, there is some Repetitious Information: beCause, no one can figure out HOW to Present a Complete Master Plan for Worldwide Law, Order, Obedience, Peace and True Prosperity, without Repeating certain Information, which is like making a Special Stew in 100 Different Ways, which everyone Loves: beCause, they are all Flavored Differently with Different Spices, in spite of having Beef, Lamb, Chicken, Turkey, Guineafowl, and Fishes of Various Kinds in them. Most of those Stews are made from Vegetables of a hundred Kinds.}

[_] 40-074 — "LIGHTNING STRIKES Versus Lightning Bugs!" (HOW you can Become Moderately RICH, without Telling any Lies nor Selling any Trash!) By The Worldwide People's Revolution!® Book 074, which is the Perfection of all of the Lightning Striking Books, which is Recommended above all others for Mass Production: beCause it stands the Best Chance of being a Real Winner, just after this Book that you are now Reading, which has a Magnetizing Title! Of course, every Book has this same Information in it: beCause, these are Advertisements for the Books, which will Naturally be Attractive to Different Kinds of Peoples: beCause, each Person has his or her Different Interests in Life. Therefore, it is Hoped that everyone will Discover a Favorite Book to Reed, and be Happy with it: beCause, all of the Books have only one Interpretation, which is that of the Inspired Author, who has Proven it, again and again, in more than 140 Inspired Books. Therefore, if anyone is Unhappy with them, let them write their own. †}

[_] 40-075 — "What are the PUNISHMENTS for Dietary Sins?" (Have we Served ourselves Well at the Tables of our Lusts?) By The Worldwide People's Revolution!® Book 075. {This Book is too Controversial to be Published at this Time. Be very Patient until it is Available: beCause it is HOT! UPDATE: This Inspired Book is now Published in several Formats. The Cheapest one is an E-Book, which might even be Free; but, the 8.5 by 11-inch Colored Edition is the Best, if you Prefer Colored Pictures, and most People do. BUT, the Black and White Edition makes a Good Gift for any Obese Person, who might be Saved by the Words of Truths within it, even if they are not Colored. A Fat Person can Skip a few Meals, just to Obtain a Colored Edition, by Saving the Money that they would spend on Eating. Our Selected King Skipped 54 Meals last October, alone.}

15

16

31

46

[_] 40-076 — "What is WRong with those CRAZY CHRISTIANS?" (A Self-Examination of the Heart of the Body of Good Government!) By The Worldwide People's Revolution!® Book 076. This Inspired Book is mostly about the Construction of our Selected King's Retirement Home, whereby they Moved no less than 66,666,666 Pounds by Hand, just to make SOLID Concrete Foundations for 40 Concrete Columns and 64 Solid Concrete Walls around 28 Concrete Floors, not Counting those in the Basement, which has 140+ Feet of Tunnels, which are Lined with Heavy Blocks. Our Selected King did most of the Work: beCause of Working on it for 6 Days per Week, and about 8 to 16 Hours per Day. It was a LOT of Fun, which he did without any Pay, nor Pains; and it is not even in his own Name! It was an Act of True Love.

[_] 40-077 — "The Gospel According to our Elected King!" (The Good News from the Most Modern Perspective!) By The Worldwide People's Revolution!® Book 077. {This is perhaps the Best Book that you will Discover on Amazon, which contains the Famous Sermon that Jonah gave to the Ninevites, plus a very Special Sermon by Jesus Christ, himself, which is taken from the Dead Sea Scrolls that were Discovered by our Selected King! It is simply a Marvelous Book that everyone must "Reed," if they Want to be Enlightened! ENJOY, and Pass it on! You and they will be Happy for it. Guaranteed! Indeed, if there is any one Book in the World, which you would Want in your Truth-brary when Jesus Returns, this one would be it. None others come Close for Originality nor Uniqueness.} †§‡

[_] 40-078 — "The Root Cause for almost all Evils!" (The Strange Things that People Say and Do to Get more Money!) By The Worldwide People's Revolution!® Book 078. {This Book contains many Colored Photographs with Fascinating Explanations! This is a Companion Book of: "For the Love of Money!" (The Strange Things that People Say and Do to Get more Money!) By The Worldwide People's Revolution!® Book 003B, which Contains the New MAGNIFIED Version of *First Timothy 6,* which has Messed Up more Minds than one could Count: beCause of being Misunderstood in all other Versions, which do not make it Clear what Ministers are supposed to Do for Money, Clothing nor Shelter. These are Minister's Favorite Books, and a Great Gift to Mankind. Be Liberated, Today!}

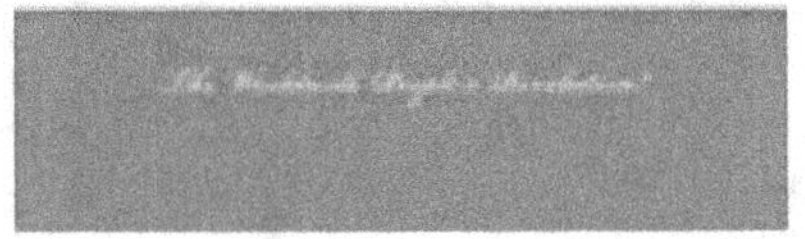

15

16

[_] 40-079 — "Orgimmick Gardening at its Best!" (HOW to Grow Delicious Satisfying Foods without a 10 Million-Dollar Investment!) By The Worldwide People's Revolution!® Book 079. {This Book also contains many Colored Photographs with Wonderful Explanations! It is a Triplet Companion Book of: "The LUSCIOUS All-Mineral Organic Method of Gardening!" (HOW to Grow DELICIOUS Satisfying Foods for Potential Kingz and Kweenz in Beautiful Swanky PALACES!) By The Worldwide People's Revolution!® Book 021B, and: "Profitable Swanky MULCHING ROCKS!" (30 Advantages for Using Swanky Mulching Rocks in an All-Mineral Organic Garden!) By The Worldwide People's Revolution!® Book 098. They are Survivalists' Books!}

30

[_] 40-080 — "Guaranteed Solutions!" (HOW to Solve our Local and Global Problems in the Most-Rational Manner Possible!) By The Worldwide People's Revolution!® Book 080. {See the Description on Amazon: because they Offer a **ONE-MILLION-DOLLAR REWARD** to anyone who can Prove our Selected King's Solutions to be WRong or Unworkable! Can you Beat that? Do you have any or all such Guaranteed Solutions? Does any Politician? Only our Selected King has those Provable Solutions: beCause God Blest him with them, which can be Proven in any Courtroom with Law and Order. ENJOY, and Pass it on! Order another one, and Reed it again for a New Experience with Greater Faith! Truths never get Tiresome, nor Boring. However, this Book does have an Error.}

43

[_] 40-081 — "Mexicans are more Intelligent than Americans!" (A Unique Challenge to all Americans and Mexicans!) By The Worldwide People's Revolution!® Book 081. {NOTE: The Remaining 275 Inspired Books by the Author of this Book may only be found in English, until we can get them Properly Translated into other Languages. Shame on you People who Killed him, who Broke his Heart with your Unbelief. May God have Mercy on your Poor Wretched Souls.} †§‡

14

[_] 40-081B — "¡Los Mexicanos son más Inteligentes que los Estadounidenses!" (¡Un Desafío Único para todos los Estadounidenses y Mexicanos!) By The Worldwide People's Revolution!® Book 082. {NOTA: Aquí está el primer Libro en Español, que puede no ser Perfecto; pero, es Perfectamente lo Suficientemente Bueno para Iluminar las Mentes de quien lo Estudia.}

29
30

[_] 40-082 — "The Process of Making a RIGHTEOUS KING!" (A Fascinating Autobiography of our Selected King!) By The Worldwide People's Revolution!® Book 082. {NOTE: He once had a 6,000-plus-page Autobiography, called: **"DIARRHEA of the Mind!"** which gave Details of his entire Life, since he was only 4 Years Old, when he had a Personal Encounter with God, which has been Lost: beCause those Backup Disks became Obsolete, and were thus Trashed, along with the Obsolete Computer, which Costed 4,000-plus Dollars, along with the Hewlett-Packard Printer, which Costed another 4,000-plus Dollars, whose Antiquated Software would not Work with a Modern Computer, nor did Hewlett have an Updated Software Program for it: beCause they are Capitalist Scammers of the Worst Kind, who should be put Out of Business for Practicing Donald Trump Tactics! See: "The Nature of CAPITALISM!" (A List of the EVILS of CAPITALISM!) By The Worldwide People's Revolution!® Book 038.}

45

[_] 40-083 — "Was Billy Graham Greatly Deceived?" (Giving Honor to whom Honor is Due!) By The Worldwide People's Revolution!® Book 083. {NOTE: If you know a Grahamite, please Direct him or her to this Inspired Book, whereby he or she might be Converted to the Truths within it, and thus be Saved from Grahamite Perversions. Thank you in Advance. They will also Thank you for it: beCause they Suffer so Needlessly, when they should be Free, Healthy and Happy, like our Selected King, who has no Aches nor Pains, who used to Work Hard all Day long, and not be Weary, just like you can Reed in *the Book of Isaiah 40:31, NMV!* Try to Find an Old Grahamite, who can Do that. God Bets that you cannot Find even ONE! Ask the Younger Grahams if they have any Aches or Pains. How will they be Saved without the Great Truths within this Inspired Book? Selah. †§‡}

16

[_] 40-084 — "The New MAGNIFIED Version of the Book of DEUTERONOMY!" (The Understandable Version of Deuteronomy in Plain English!) Book 084. This is actually one of the Best Books within the entire *Holy Bible,* and also one of the Longest; but, do not allow that Fact to Deter you by any Means: beCause, "the Bigger Book is Normally a Better Book," which is True of a lot of Books, including all of the above Books: beCause it is the Nature of the Holy Spirit to get into Long-winded Sermons, you might say, which is WHY the Apostle Paul Preached until Midnight in *the Book of Acts,* until some Boy went to Sleep and Fell from a Window and Killed himself, whom the Apostle Paul Raised Up from the Dead and went on Preaching until the Dawn of the Day! And it is NOT Jewish Mythology! †§‡§§ {See: "The New MAGNIFIED Version of the Book of ACTS" for the Finest of Details, B63.}

29
30

[_] 40-085 — "All of the Arguments are in Favor of our Selected King, who has Zero Challengers!" (Before you Attend another Election Deception, you should Carefully Study this Inspired Book with an Honest Open Mind!) By The Worldwide People's Revolution!® Book 085. There are Better Books; but, not very many of them. No Wicked Politician can Handle this one without EXPLODING all over the Place! §‡

44

[_] 40-086 — "Provable Truths that True Christians cannot Rightly Deny!" (A Fair Challenge for all Professing "Christians" to Meditate on with Honest Open Minds!) By The Worldwide People's Revolution!® Book 086. It makes a Nice Gift for Professing "Christians," who still have something to Learn.

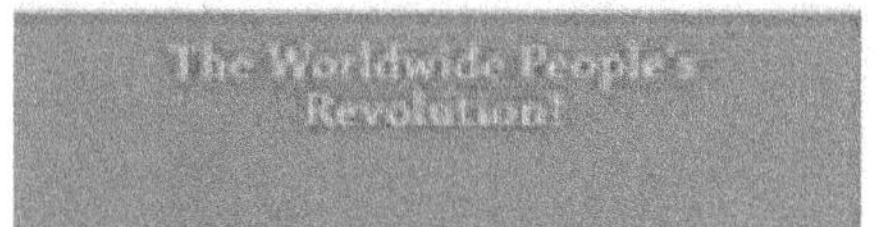

[_] 40-087 — "How all Women can Get True Justice without Getting Divorced from God!" (The Unjust Case of Judge Brett Kavanaugh and Doctor Christine Blasey Ford is now Revisited by a Wise Son of King Solomon!) By The Worldwide People's Revolution!® Book 087. The Judge would have to Resign from the Low Court of Supreme Injustices, if he should Happen to Reed this Inspired Book. You could Send a Copy to him for Christmas. But, do not Expect any Appreciation for it: beCause he is Obviously Caught between a Rock of Provable Truths, and a Hard Place in "The Low Court of Supreme Injustices is Brought to Trial!" (Our Selected King Butts Heads with the United States Supreme Court, with or without their Black Robes of Hypocrisies and Lies!) By The Worldwide People's Revolution!® Book 011B. (Yes, I Know, it did not quite Work Out Correctly, did it? Sorry.)

[_] 40-088 — "The New MAGNIFIED Version of GENESIS!" (The Enlightening Version of the Beginnings of Things!) By The Worldwide People's Revolution!® Book 088. Actually, no one Knows for Sure what Happened in the so-called "Beginning," which has no Date on it; but, it was most Certainly NOT 6,000 Years Ago: beCause there are Prehistoric Fossils on the Top of Mount Everest, and any of them are Older than Father Adam! But, you are Welcome to Believe whatever you Like, and it will not Change the Facts by even one Degree. Chances are that Adam was put here LONG after the Earth was Inhabited by Aliens from other Worlds. In Fact, God would likely Bet on it! You would also likely Bet on it. Everyone with an Education would likely Bet on it. But, none of it Matters as much as the Provable Truths within this Inspired Book.

[_] 40-089 — "The New MAGNIFIED Version of the HOLY KORAN!" (WHY MuhamMAD went to Hell for Spiritual MURDER!) By The Worldwide People's Revolution!® Book 089. This is by Far the Best Version of the *Holy Koran,* which is Loved by all Honest Muslims, Hindus, Christians and Buddhists, Worldwide! Surprise yourself and others. Ask them what it Means? Just Open it at Random, and Reed the first Words that your Eyes Land on, and See for yourself that it Speaks with your Heart and Mind, which should be in Perfect Agreement, if Things are Correct, as they should be, and as they will be, if you Love and Obey ALL that is GOOD, which is GOD. Just be Patient until **"The GWTCH!"** Book 041B. *"Prove all Provable Things, and Cling Tightly to ALL that is GOOD." — Holy Scripture.* †§‡

1

16

31

40

[ ] 40-090 — **"A New Jerusalem in the Great State of Flexible Texas!" (HOW to make Good Use of the Mississippi River!) By The Worldwide People's Revolution!® Book 090.** This Inspired Book contains many Fascinating Photos of God's Handiwork. ENJOY! It also Contains Inspired Words that you have never Heard before! Do not be Afraid of them: beCause, they will not Bite you, nor Pervert your Mind in any Way. God is Able and Willing to Help you to Understand all such Words, even if you Presently Understand nothing. Just have enough Faith to Reed it, one Time, and you will no doubt be Captivated by it, and in a Good Way, for which you will be Happy for it. After all, our Selected King is the Healthiest and Happiest Man that you could ever Meet, who is Free from all Pains and Sufferings. Selah. †§‡

[ ] 40-091 — **"What is The GREATEST SIN?" (And it is NOT Blasphemy Against the Holy Spirit!) By The Worldwide People's Revolution!® Book 091.** Most People have no Idea what the Greatest Sin might be; but, it is the Sin that Causes almost all of the other Sins. CLUE: It is something that most People Commit every Day of their Liivz; but, they do not Know it. Moreover, it Keeps them in the Darkness of Ignorance, whereby they cannot Discover the Key of the Nolij of All that is Good and Evil, whereby they might Unlock the Door of Confession, and Escape from their Prison of Lies. Therefore, if you Reed this Book, do not Reject any Provable Truth within it, lest you should never Escape from your own Prison of Sins. Be Perfectly Honest and Open-Minded. Selah.

[ ] 40-092 — **"HOW to Make America (and all other Nations) Really GREAT Without Telling any LIES!" (The Founding Fathers would have Loved it!) By The Worldwide People's Revolution!® Book 092.** The Fake Trumpeter was going to "Make America Great Again," according to his Campaign Banner; but, instead of doing that, he made Americans more Divided and Confused than ever. Indeed, instead of becoming ONE with God, in Mind, Spirit and Body, Americans are on the Verge of some Strange Uncivilized WAR! So, how can they be Saved from their Madness and Divisions? This Inspired Book Reveals HOW, WHY, WHEN and Where, O Lady Doubtfulness. Your Children will no doubt Love it; but, only after **"The Great ATOMIC NIGHTMARE!" (The Saddest Story in World History!) By The Great White Bald Eagle! Book 099.** You can Blame the Fake Snooze Reporters. ‡

1

16

31

46

[_] 40-093 — "HOW Righteousness can Overcome Wickedness!" (The Triumph of the Soul who Knows God!) By The Enlightened Professor of Common Sense! Book 093. {Notice how the Calves in the Cover Photo Segregated themselves by their Colors, from Left to Right. God Guided them for a Perfect Picture; and it is not the First Time that I have gotten a Perfect Picture. You have probably Experienced Similar Things. But, it is the Expressions on their Faces, which make the Photo Extra Special. Therefore, go to www.Amazon.com and Check them out for yourself. Look at the hundreds of Photos in the Books. Read the Explanations for them, and Meditate on them: beCause, it is True that a Picture can be Worth 10,000 Words. ‡}

[_] 40-094 — "Justifications for MAGNIFICATIONS!" (The Problem with Understanding a Complicated Contradictory Mutilated Unholy Bible!) Or: (The Problem with Inventing Lies that are too BIG to DIE!) By The Worldwide People's Revolution!® Book 094. Children should not be overly Discouraged by the Multitude of Contradictions within the so-called "Holy Bible," beCause the New MAGNIFIED Version makes most of it Perfectly Clear: beCause, it is a Revelation from God, who Knows the Truth of it in all Cases, who Permitted those Contradictions, just to Test our Faith in Provable Truths, which can also be Found within those Pages. Therefore, we must Learn to Separate Truths from Lies: beCause, there are also a LOT of Lies within that so-called "Holy Bible"! Yes, you can Discover some of them in:

[_] 40-095 — "HOW to IDENTIFY God's Elected Ones!" (Are YOU one of the Elect?) By The Worldwide People's Revolution!® Book 095. {It seems that if you are among "the Elect," you have nothing to Worry about: beCause, you are "Saved," and going to "Heaven" when you Die — that is, IF you Actually "Die." Many Professing "Christians" Actually Believe that they will NOT Die, no matter what: beCause, "they are Alive in Christ, even if they are Rotted," as one sed it. Well, their Faith is Commendable; but, is it Reliable? What if they are only Deceived by their Fake Faith? After all, it is Difficult to Believe that 10,000 False Religions could all be Correct about their Contradictory Beliefs. But, you are Welcome to Believe whatever you Like; and it always Sounds Good to be on God's Side of every Issue, even if it has no Credibility at all. †§‡§§}

[_] 40-096 — "GOVERNMENT Versus Independence!" (How Much CONTROL Should a Government Have?") By The Worldwide People's Revolution!® Book 096. {When People have Freedom to Say and Do whatever they Want to, we just Naturally get a Big Disorganized Mess like New Yuck City, Chicago, Lost Angels, Californicate, or Bombay, India, where People are running around like Chickens with their Heads Chopped Off, or Maggots Crawling around in and over a Dead Carcass. The Stink is almost Unbearable. So, just how Much CONTROL should a Government have? Should the People be FORCED to Follow the Dictates of "TYRANTS"? The Communists Tested their Versions of Prosperity, and Failed. The Socialists Tested their Versions, and Failed. And the Capitalists Managed to Produce Millions of Criminals. None of them Produced Healthy nor Happy People. Almost all of them Liv in Ugly Painted Houses, like Rats and Slaves in Cages, who are somewhat Contented, if their Bellies are Full. †§‡}

[_] 40-097 — "C-SPAN-DEX!" (Your Filtered View of Bad Government!) By The Worldwide People's Revolution!® Book 097. {This Inspired Book contains the entire Orlando, Florida, President Donald Trump Campaign Speech, along with our Selected King's Corrections and Improvements, plus a lot of other Appropriate Information for an Election Year. You can read a lot of Free Pages on Amazon for Encouragement. It is Really GOOD! Just be Patient about reading it: beCause, the Campaign Speech is as Boring as Mud in a Barnyard, even if you can Manage to Wade through it in your Tall Insulated Red-Rubber Hip Boots. If the Electors had red this Inspired Book, before the Election Deception, the Fake Trumpeter would most likely have Received no more than a few thousand Votes, and only from the most Ignorant Fools. †§‡}

[_] 40-098 — "Profitable Swanky MULCHING ROCKS!" (30 Advantages for Using Swanky Mulching Rocks in an All-Mineral Organic Garden!) By The Worldwide People's Revolution!® Book 098. {Just Think, the School of Fools never Mentioned them, nor did the False Governments, nor did any of the False Churches: beCause they are simply Uneducated and Foolish, who are not even Looking for Ways to make the Masses of People Richer. This is a Companion Book of: "The LUSCIOUS All-Mineral Organic Method of Gardening!" (HOW to Grow DELICIOUS Satisfying Foods for Potential Kingz and Kweenz in Beautiful Swanky PALACES!) By The Worldwide People's Revolution!® Book 021B, and: "Orgimmick Gardening at its Best!" (HOW to Grow Delicious Satisfying Foods without a 10 Million-Dollar Investment!) By The Worldwide People's Revolution!® Book 079.}

[_] 40-099 — "The Great ATOMIC NIGHTMARE!" (The Saddest Story in World History!) By The Great White Bald Eagle! Book 099. {NOTE: Let us Hope and Pray that no one ever has to Write this Book; but, if they Do, it should Spook the Devil Out of you!} This Book comes in 5 Different Versions, if you can Find them. Amazon seems to be Reluctant to Publish them. I Wonder why

7

[_] 40-100 — "Our Selected King SPEAKS OUT!" (It is High Time for some Sane Person to get Total Control of this Insane World!) By The Worldwide People's Revolution!® Book 100!

11

15

28

[_] 40-101 — "What will you Do when the Rain STOPS?" (God's Last Resort to Save Mankind from his MADNESS!) By The Worldwide People's Revolution!® Book 101! {One might Think that an All-Powerful God would have a Better Remedy for what Ails Mankind, than Stopping the Rain, and Starving the People and Animals and Plants; but, that is the Best Remedy that God can Think of, which Readjusts the Population Growth, and Reduces the Numbers of Sick and Degenerated Creatures, while Strengthening the Remaining ones, which has Worked quite Well for thousands of Years. After all, when there is nothing to Eat nor Drink, what else can we Do, except to Fast and Pray, which Rearranges our Brains and Bodies, and gets Rid of a LOT of Accumulated FILTH and Stink, which is also True for many Sicknesses and Diseases, which are Natural House-cleaning Programs, you might say, as Harsh as they are, even as Deadly as some of them are, which are Necessary.}

[_] 40-102 — "Beautiful Swanky Stone Dome Home COMPLEXES!" (HOW to Build SECURE Tax-proof, Insurance-proof, Self-air-conditioned, Paint-proof, Rot-proof, Termite-proof, Mouse-proof, Fireproof, Tornado-proof, Hurricane-proof, Thief-proof, and BOMB-PROOF Houses!) By The Worldwide People's Revolution!® Book 102. The 8.5 by 11-inch Colored Edition is by far the Best Edition, if you can find it. Hunt for this ISBN: 978-1689-4295-04.

[_] 40-103 — "Royal Swanky Buffets!" (The Best Feasts in the Whole World!) By The Worldwide People's Revolution!® Book 103. {Swanky Fortresses are Designed for SURVIVAL, which Naturally Includes a Good Reliable Food Supply and Water Supply. Therefore, you can Expect to See hundreds of Royal Swanky Buffets within each Large Swanky Fortress, which might bc 20 to 200 Miles in Diameter, and Built Up in as many as 66 Great Stone TERRACES with Swanky Stone Dome Homes under those Terraced Gardens, Vineyards, and Orchards: beCause, each Terrace will be about 240 Feet WIDE, and Miles Long, which will make a Spectacular Sight from any Angle or Viewpoint; but, especially from the Swanky Castle Towers at the Corners, where a Person might See as many as 666 Great Stone Terraces, including those of the Hotel, Castle and Fortress, since the Castle is Extra Tall, which would have Telescopes for getting Better Views; but, the Royal Swanky Buffets would be the Primary Attractions in most Swanky Fortresses: beCause of having a thousand or more Dishes of Delicious Foods to Choose from, which come from all around the World! You must Taste! †§‡}

[_] 40-104 — "101 Good Reasons and Great Advantages for Establishing a Righteous One-World Government!" (Government By the People, Of the People, and For the People!) By The Worldwide People's Revolution!® Book 104. This Book Suggests thousands of Good Reasons and Great Advantages. But, of course, you have to be Able to THINK, in order to get the Full Implications of it, which seems to be something that Wicked Politicians cannot Do, or Refuse to Do; and neither can most Preachers and Teachers Do it. Therefore, this Inspired Book will Help them to Think and Remember what they already Know, just from Watching Evening Snooze Reports on TV, which Constantly Remind us of Natural Disasters, which can be Prevented by Building Secure Swanky Hotels, Castles and Fortresses, which have more than 5,000 Advantages over Cities of Confusion, Crime, Pollution, Protests, Riots, Luting, Burning, and so on. Just Study it for yourself.

[_] 40-105 — "The New MAGNIFIED Version of the Book of REVELATION!" (The Understandable Version of the Most-Controversial Book in the Whole World!) By The Worldwide People's Revolution!® Book 105. This Proverbial "Bombshell" will be Published just before the Second Coming of Jesus Christ! Get your Seatbelts Fastened! Be Prepared for Radical Changes, Worldwide: beCause, Satan is Coming with his Seven Last Great Plagues, and you are most apt to be Caught right in the Middle of it! But, no one would have to Suffer, if they were just Humble and Perfectly Honest about all Things: beCause, our Selected King Reveals HOW we can all Escape from the Great Tribulation, and even Flourish during the Great 3.5-year Worldwide FAMINE, just by Building those "GLORIOUS Swanky Hotels Castles and Fortresses!" (Beautiful Planned City States for WISE Intelligent Well-Educated People with Common Sense and Good Understanding!) By The Worldwide People's Revolution!® Book 019B.

[_] 40-106 — "The Naked Glory of Beautiful Mankind!" (1,000 Pages of Sheer Artistic BEAUTY!) By The Worldwide People's Revolution!® Book 106. (See Book 014B-02-09-T for the Explanation.)

[_] 40-107 — "The Beautiful Faces of Holy Men!" (The very Best that God has to Offer!) By The Worldwide People's Revolution!® Book 107. {NOTE: If you know of any Holy Men, please Kindly Ask them if you can get their Photograph, and E-mail it to the Address on the Outside of the Back Cover of this Book, which is near to the Bottom of the Page. When we get enough of those Pictures, we will make up a Book for our Readers. You may Write whatever Information that you know about them, with their Approval. We must Know that they Approve of it: beCause, we are not Trying to Embarrass anyone; but, only let People Know what Holy Men Look Like, whereby they might also be Inspired to become Like them. Chances are that Body Builders will be the Most Attractive; but, the Faces of Holy Men are the Most Beautiful and Praiseworthy. †§‡}

15

[ ] 40-108 — "The Worldwide People's Revolution!" (A Comprehensive Plan for Obtaining Worldwide Law, Order, Obedience, Peace and True Prosperity!) By The Worldwide People's Revolution!® Book 108. {Anyone and Everyone is Welcome to Join **The Worldwide People's Revolution,** which is Seeking to Right the Wrongs, and make this a Good World for everyone to Liv in, including the Animals, who have been Greatly Abused by Capitalism, which Takes Away; but, Rarely Gives Back. **The Worldwide People's Revolution** is Seeking to Built Up a Righteous Empire with a One-World Government with Limited Powers: beCause, each Beautiful Planned City State will Govern itself; but, with the HELP of a Good Federal Government, which has an Unlimited Supply of Good Money, which must be EARNED by Honest Labor, and Represented by Things of True Value. Selah. †‡}

[ ] 40-109 — "VOTE for The GOAT!" (The New Political Party that has Guaranteed Solutions for our Massive Problems!) By The Worldwide People's Revolution!® Book 109. {Of course, the Election Deception has Come and Gone; but, we can well Believe that another one will soon be here: beCause Time Moves by so Swiftly, and especially when we are Busy; and our Selected King has been Extra Busy with Great ZEAL for what is Riit: beCause God has Blest him with "Guaranteed Solutions!" (HOW to Solve our Local and Global Problems in the Most-Rational Manner Possible!) By The Worldwide People's Revolution!® Book 080. Therefore, it is up to the Electors to Study those Solutions, and **VOTE for The GOAT,** who is the Scapegoat, or the one whom we can all Blame, if anything goes WRong under his Administration, who must be the Most-Righteous Man among us. However, if you

30   Disagree with that Statement, please E-mail your Better Suggestion to the Address on the Back.‡}

31

[ ] 40-110 — "IMPORTANT THINGS that Should Have Been Written in the Holy Bible!" (A Special Challenge to all Professing Christians, Jews, Hindus, Muslims and Atheists!) **By** The Irreverent Penname Scumbag! Book 110. {The so-called *"Holy Bible"* does not even Reveal where to Obtain the Necessary Money for Operating a Good Government. It just Assumes that everyone already Knows where to Obtain that Money, from Mining for Gold, Silver, and other Precious Metals; but, is that HOW God would have us Do it? This Inspired Book Presents a FAR Superior Plan for Obtaining an Endless Supply of Good Money, which must be EARNED by Honest Labor, without any Loans, without any Interest and without any Hateful Taxes! Such Information cannot be Found in any Unholy Mutilated Bibles. Guaranteed! ‡}

[ ] 40-111 — "Hosts of HOAXES Live In Under Around and Over the Little White OUTHOUSE!" (WHY Spiritually-Blind Cowardly-Americans are Hunkering Down in their Empty Root Cellars!) **By The Irreverent Penname Oversight!** Book 111. {The Bug-19 made its Attack in the Year of our Grand Deceptions 2020. It has already Killed more than a Million People, and has no Intentions of taking a Rest, which is a Great Challenge to all of Mankind, which can easily be Defeated by People who Fast and Pray: beCause, the Human Body, and all other Bodies of Flesh, are Designed to Heal themselves, which you can Prove for yourself, just by Cutting your own Finger with a Knife. However, when we Stop Eating and take a Fast, it Speeds Up the Healing Processes: beCause, the Energy that would Normally be Spent on Digesting Foods and Poisonous Drinks, can now be Used to Heal us.}

18

[ ] 40-112 — "Should Wives Obey their Husbands?" (OR, Should Husbands OBEY their Wives?) **By The Irreverent Penname Mockingbird!** Book 112. {You might Think that this would be a very Controversial Book: beCause of bringing up the Issue of "Male versus Female" Thing. However, you never did See a Female Elk Butting Heads with a Male Elk: beCause, Strangely enough, ALL Wild Females Know their Rightful Place in this World, and leave the "Politics" to the Stronger Sex, who Play their Butting Heads Game, just to Discover WHO is in Charge of Things. Our Selected King Challenges Everyone.}

30

125

1

[ ] 40-113 — "Modern Deceived SLAVES!" (10 Simple Steps for Liberating ALL Modern Slaves, Worldwide, Including Yourself!) **By Liberty and Justice for ALL!** Book 113. {The 8.5 by 11-inch Colored Edition is Best, if you can Find it. We cannot. Someone at Amazon is rather Lazy, I would say. Just WHY they do not Want People to Discover the 8.5 by 11-inch Colored Edition is a Mystery, since it is by Far the Superior Book with Line Numbers, Large-easy-to-Reed Print, Large Pictures and Screen Shots. Perhaps they Imagine that most People cannot Afford such a Book, which has more than 60 Colored Photographs? Well, those same People seem to Afford Expensive Meals, which Disappear within an Hour or less, while an Exceptionally Good Book like this one will be around for Decades to come, if it is taken Good Care of, which even the Great Grandchildren can Feast on. Therefore, this seems to be the Wiser Investment for Satisfied Minds. But, if you Doubt it, just Reed the Free Book Preview on Amazon.}

[ ] 40-114 — "Are you a Jobless Graduate of the School of Fools?" (How to Obtain a Good Education without Robbing the Bank, Selling any Trash, nor Telling any Lies!) **By The Professor Wordcraft Enlightenment!** Book 114. {We all most likely know someone, who is tens of thousands of Dollars in Debt for their so-called "Education," who were Persuaded by the Long Unemployment Lines that they must get a "Good Education" by going into Debt to the Devil, when no such Debts are Needed, nor is the Devil Needed for True Prosperity; but, a Righteous Government is Needed, and it has an Unlimited Supply of Good Money, which must be EARNED by Honest Labor, without any Loans, without any Interest, and without any Hateful Taxes! BUT, you might Ask, "WHO Pays for the Highways and Bridges in such a Government?" Answer: The Good Government, which has a Good Supply of Good Money, which must be EARNED by Honest Labor, even as we already Stated. However, the Mountains of Rocks are FREE, just like Sunlight and Rainwater, which Belong to GOD, who has Generously GIVEN them to ALL of us, and Kindly Asked us to SHARE them with one another, as Brothers and Sisters might Do, if they Truly Loved one another. However, we must Use those Mountains of Rocks WISELY, and get everyone Set Up Properly in their own Private Gardens of Eden, whereby every Family can Feed and Clothe itself, without Depending on Welfare Checks, Food Stamps, nor Handouts from Poor Naaberz, who have NO Gardens to Work in, who are also Relying on a Great False Economy, which can Quickly become another Great DEPRESSION, whereby most of the People are Unemployed, or even HOMELESS! Yes, Millions of People are now Living on the Streets, for the Lack of "Seven Great Armies of Working Soldiers!" (HOW to Provide a Way for Everyone to WORK: so as to Eliminate Poverty, Crimes, Drug Abuses, Prisons and Unnecessary Taxes!) By The Worldwide People's Revolution!® Book 015B. Therefore, it is now Time for Everyone to STUDY those Provable TRUTHS, and Stop Lying to themselves! †‡}

[_] 40-115 — "Beautiful Swanky FASTING SANITARIUMS!" (HOW to Learn Good Self-Discipline!) **By The Worldwide People's Revolution!®** Book 115. {If you have ever Attempted to Do any Fasting, you have most likely Discovered that there is no Good Place to Do it, nor anyone to Help you to Do it, which Moses also Discovered when he went up on Mount Sinai, when he was 80 Years Old; but, Joshua Volunteered to Help him take Enemas (which Part was Deleted by the Edomites, who did not Want anyone to Discover the Great Benefits of Enemas, when People get Old and Weak while Fasting: beCause, like Medical Snakes, they Wanted to Sell Drugs). Therefore, the Solution is to Build …}

13

14
15

[_] 40-116 — "Swanky Institutions for Compassionate Corrections!" (How to Correct even the Most-Stubborn Bullies!) **By The Biggest Bully of All Bullies!** Book 116. {Medical Doctors Know for a Fact that the Accumulated Filth within the Bowels of Criminals (including the Chief Criminals in Washington, District of Criminals) is to be Blamed for Producing Criminals: beCause, when those Poisons and Filth are Removed by Fasting, the "Demons" Depart, which anyone can also Prove for himself, just by Fasting and Praying. Therefore, Tyrant Governments — such as the Former Union of Soviet Socialistic Republicans (USSR) — Forced People to FAST on Meager Rations of Turnips and Wild Onions, just to Accomplish that Goal of Removing the "Demons," which they Discovered by Chance. However, there was no Compassion nor Love in it, which we now Know are Necessary for Success: beCause, People must Know that they are Loved, which they will Discover at **Swanky Institutions for Compassionate Corrections!** Therefore, let Nature take its Course. Selah. §‡}

33

34

15

[_] 40-117 — "What is True PROGRESS???" (Are we Making any True Progress, at all?) By The Worldwide People's Revolution!® Book 117. {The Divided States of United Lies has Millions of Prisoners, and Millions of Potential Criminals, who are only Restrained by their FEARS of Losing their Freedoms to Eat and Drink at the Death and Hell Restaurants. In other Words, it is NOT a Success Story by any Means: beCause, all of those Criminals were Produced by an Evil Thing called "CAPITALISM," which is the Root Cause for most Evils in this World of Woes: beCause, it is the Love of Money in Action! But, not everyone is Willing to Play by the Capitalist Rules: beCause, it is Conveniently easy to Cheat in one Way or another, which Weak-minded People just Naturally Do, and often end up in Prisons for it. So, what is the Best Solution? Read the Book, and do not Forget to Pass it on to other Victims of Capitalism.}

16

[_] 40-118 — "Is America a White Nation with a Black Heart?" (How to Separate Truth from Fiction!) By The Good Pastor of Uncommon Sense! Book 118. {Of course, the Answer to the Question is a Resounding, NO! Americans are Victims of Satan, the Devil, who has Deceived them with a Pack of Capitalist Lies, which is Based on *the Love of Money,* which is the Root Cause for most Evils; but, not ALL Evils, as in the Case of the Murder of George Floyd, which was an Obvious Case of Racial Hate and Discrimination: beCause of the Color of the Man's Skin, which made him "one of them," and not "one of us." George could have Fought Back; but, he was a Humble Submissive Person, who was simply Abused by a White Nigger with a Black Heart, who is likely to be Born in some African Jungle the next Time Around, where he will have Time to Think about it. What do you Think? †§‡}

32

[_] 40-119 — "Which Church is the Right Church?" (Can all Churches be Correct?) By The Good Pastor of Uncommon Sense! Book 119. {There are more than 10,000 Varieties of "Christian" Churches in this World of Woes, which Means that if any one of them has the Riit Doctrines, all of the others must have WRong Doctrines: beCause, there is no Way that ALL of them could be Exactly RIIT, seeing that they have Contradictory Doctrines. Therefore, which Church is the Right Church? Well, this Inspired Book Investigates the Possibility that they are ALL WRong; but, that is not to say that at least one of them might be Riit, which is Naturally the Church that our Selected King Belongs to: beCause, he Accepts the Provable Truths from ALL Religions, and only those. †§‡}

[_] 40-120 — "Do People Go to Heaven when they Die?" (The Unbelievable Truth about Life and Death!) **By The Good Pastor of Uncommon Sense!** Book 120. {It is a very Common Belief among almost all Religions, that People go to Heaven when they Die, and especially if they have been "Good People," who did not Use God's Name in Vain with Cursing, nor Murdered anyone with a Meat Cleaver; but, it was Permissible for them to Drop Bombs on the Designated "Enemies," or Blast them Away with Land Mines, Grenades, or Napalm — just as long as they are Doing it in the Holy Names of Demon-ocracy, Freedom, Liberty, and Justice for ALL, as Satan might say. So, what is the Truth of it — Do People go to Heaven when they Die, or not? Well, this Inspired Book Presents MOUNTAINS of Evidences that they do NOT! But, of course, that is a Bit of an Exaggeration, you might say: beCause, there is not even ONE such Cemetery, nor Hill of Evidences; but, there are lots of *Biblical* Evidences. †§‡§§}

18

[_] 40-121 — "The Hopeless Church of Little Faith!" (The Unholy Church of Graceful Sinners, who are Mostly just Liars and Hypocrites!) **By The Good Pastor of Uncommon Sense!** Book 121. {X-number of People are Offended by the Title of the Book, alone, without Reading the entire Book: beCause, they Belong to the Hopeful Church of Great Faith, which has no Doubts about them not going to Heaven when they Die: beCause, they have been "SAVED," if you can Believe it; but, NOT Saved from any of their Sins, which are Transgressions of God's Laws, which they simply Ignore: beCause, "the law was crucified with Christ," they say; but, behold, the Laws and Commandments of Christ were NOT Crucified with him, or else there was no Use for Giving them! Why even Mention them, if they were Done Away with? Indeed, it is all just another Biblical Contradiction for the Sake of Religious Confusion, which Satan LOVES, and much more than you might Imagine: beCause, he is the Father of all Lies and Deceptions, who Seeks to Obtain as many Souls as Possible for his own Unholy Kingdom, which is a False Government of Outlandish LIES, which were mostly Inventions of the JEWS, Muslims, Hindus, and Professing CHRISTIANS, who are Naturally the most easily Deceived: beCause of Assuming that their Traditional Religious Upbringing was Exactly RIGHT, which is WHY that their Parents Accepted it to Begin with, and then Tawt their False Religion to THEM, which is always Based on whatever the *"Holy Bible"* has to Teach about it — except that the so-called *"holy Bible"* is Missing several Good Books, which it Mentions! But, of course, those Professing "Christians" never red enough of it to Discover any of those Missing Books, nor the 3,000 or more Missing Books that are NOT Mentioned by it, which Contradict Vain Traditional Religious Teachings! So, WHO is Riit, and WHO is WRong? For Sure, the Liars and Hypocrites cannot be Riit. Only Saints could be. †§‡§§}

[_] 40-122 — "HOW to Make Proper REPARATIONS!" (True Justice for Black and White People, and Everyone in Between them!) **By** The Worldwide People's Revolution!® Book 122. (This Book was Inspired by: https://youtu.be/QOPGpE-sXh0 The Truth about the Confederacy in the United States | Full Version.) {Of course, all of the Readers, except for ONE, have just Naturally Assumed what this Inspired Book is all about — REPARATIONS! But, this is a Great REVOLUTIONARY Plan for Proper Reparations for EVERYONE: beCause, all Peoples have been Greatly Abused, and not just Black Peoples, nor Poor Brown Peoples; but, EVERY PERSON on the Whole Earth, who has been Deprived of those "Beautiful Swanky PALACES!" (A New Concept in Living Habits — Swanky Palaces for Poor People!) By The Worldwide People's Revolution!® Book 066. Therefore, Feel Sorry for yourself, if you Will: beCause, you are one of them! SELAH. ‡}

[_] 40-123 — "What would Moses and Jesus Do with the Statues and Monuments???" (A Unique Plan for Solving the Problem, which Everyone can be Extra Happy with!) **By** Liberty and Justice is for ALL! Book 123. {If there is any one Thing that gets under the Thin Skin of Idol Worshipers, it is the Destruction of their Idols. For Example, Laban Chased after Jacob in *Genesis 31,* in order to Recover the Idols that were Stolen from him by Rachel, who Hid them among the "Furniture" of her Camel, and Sat on them for Security: beCause, at that Time, Women were not Required to Dismount from their Camels, if they Wanted to Sit Tight; but, Laban was very Upset over his Idols, even as many Americans are Upset over the Destruction of their Idols and the Memories of their Heroes. So, is there any "Middle Ground" to Stand on, whereby everyone can be made Happy by it? Well, our Selected King has Discovered a Wise Solution for it, which every Sane Person can Cheerfully Agree with: beCause, everyone will be Able to Keep their Idols, and Babysit them, you might say, and not even Jehovah God will be Unhappy with that Plan: beCause, he Allows that most People are Crazy, if not all of them! After all, what Idol is as Good as a Real Person. For Example, would you Prefer that Jesus Christ should Appear in PERSON, or Send an Idol of himself to Comfort you? Of course, the Real Person would be much more Appreciated; but, for some Strange Reason, he seems to be Unable or Unwilling to Appear in Person, whereby all Important Issues might be Settled: beCause, he could Settle them with his own Sword of Truths, if he has one; and, we are Assured in *the Book of Revelation* that the Double-Edged Sword of Truth comes Out of his own Mouth, which anyone can Discover in Chapter 1, Verse 16. Therefore, he has such a Sword; but, at this Time he is simply Unwilling to Use it: beCause, he is Trying to Discover his True Followers, who must be Tested in a Furnace of Affliction for their Goodness. Where do you Think that you will Stand during his Judgment Day — Inside or Outside of the Bounds of the Law? Moreover, will it be the *Old Testament Laws,* or the *New Testament Laws* that we will be Judged by? Does it Matter which Laws? If so, what about OUR Laws and Rules? †§‡}

[ ] 40-124 — "Belgiculture!" (A Complete Master Plan for Solving the Countless Problems of Mankind!) **By** The Worldwide People's Revolution!® Belgique Book 124. {This is a Special Book for Special People, which is a Good Book to Give to a Potential Friend as a GIFT: beCause, it is full of Pictures with Enlightening Explanations, which most People (and ALL Honest People) will Cheerfully Agree with, which is WHY that most Europeans Love it. After all, no one in his nor her Riit Mind can Argue Against BELGICULTURE, which is the Culture of "The New RIGHTEOUS One-World Government!" (HOW to Establish a Righteous One-World Government without Going to WAR!) By The Worldwide People's Revolution!® Book 056, which Believes that everyone should be FORTIFIED and Secure at HOME. But, you are Welcome to Present to us your Honest Opinions and Arguments.}

[ ] 40-125 — "Good Lessons for Honest Wise Men!" (A Simplistic Plan for Totally Solving the Complicated Problems of Deceived Mankind!) **By** The Smarter Professor of Common Sense! Book 125. {This Book is just another Better Version of Belgiculture, which is more Magnified, you might say; but, it is Basically the same Book, which a Smarter Professor Improved on. In other Words, there are probably a thousand or more Different Ways to Present the same Good Message, and one of those Ways is Destined to be Accepted by Thinking People with Common Sense. After all, there are more than 5,000 Good Reasons and Great Advantages for Building those "GLORIOUS Swanky Hotels Castles and Fortresses!" (Beautiful Planned City States for WISE Intelligent Well-Educated People with Common Sense and Good Understanding!) By The Worldwide People's Revolution!® Book 019B. None will be just Alike. †§‡}

[ ] 40-126 — "The Sixth Book of Moses, called: GOOD GOVERNMENT!" (The Primary Missing Book in the Holy Bible!) **By** The Worldwide People's Revolution!® Book 126. {Some People are so Superstitious that they Sincerely Believe that their Personal God Wrote every Word in the *King James Version of the Holy Bible,* which does not make much Sense to the Translators of it, who Confessed that they Added no less than 10,000 *Italicized Words,* themselves, just to make it a little more Understandable. But, after Reading that so-called *"Holy Bible"* from Cover to Cover, and more than 20 Times, our Selected King came to Realize that the Holy Spirit, alone, can be Trusted, and only IF a Person has Pure Thots. Therefore, his New MAGNIFIED Version (NMV) of it, is Far more Accurate than any other Version, which can be Proven in a Courtroom, if anyone is Interested in it; and all Atheists shoud be.}

[_] 40-127 — "Election Deceptions Versus True Prosperity!" (Provable Truths that Young People can Believe in!) **By The Professor of Reason and Logic!** Book 127. {This Inspired Book is Designed Especially for Young People, who cannot Visualize a Happy Future for themselves: beCause, they are made into Debt Slaves before they even Graduate from the School of Fools. Indeed, they will no doubt be the First to Join **"The Swanky Associations of Working Soldiers!" (A Fascinating Collection of Various Kinds of Voluntary Working Soldiers!) By The Worldwide People's Revolution!®** Book 018B, whereby they can do so little as 4 Hours of Common Skilled Labor per Workday, and Liv within those "Beautiful Swanky PALACES!" (A New Concept in Living Habits — Swanky Palaces for Poor People!) By The Worldwide People's Revolution!® Book 066, within about 6 Years. Selah. ‡}

15

[_] 40-128 — "Conspiracy Theories did it!" (The Evil Events of September 11th 2001 are Revisited by a Wise Son of King Solomon!) **By** The Worldwide People's Revolution!® Book 128. {Most Americans have already Concluded that Conspiracy Theories did it; but, take a Good Honest Look at that Sliced-Off Hardened-Steel Column, and Ask yourself: "WHO could have Done that?" Well, you can be Sure that "Conspiracy Theories" never did it, nor did any Airplanes, Hijackers with Box Cutters, nor even the Gestapo SS Storm Troopers of the Right Wing Neo-Nazi Party; but, some American-Israeli Demolition Team must have Done it: beCause, there are only 6 such Demolition Teams in the Whole World, and they are ALL Israeli-Based Teams, who alone have the Expertise to Do it, which must be Proven in a Courtroom, O Leapfrogs. So, are you Willing to Call for **"The GWTCH,"** O you Spiritual Cowards?}

30

[_] 40-129 — "Justifications for Writing Styles!" (Why our Selected King Writes so Strangely!) By The Worldwide People's Revolution!® Book 129. {You have probably Noticed that our Selected King Capitalizes a LOT of Important Words, which is not Traditional; but, it was Traditional during the not-too-distant Past, during the Days of the Founding Fathers of "The Divided States of United Lies!" (The so-called "United States of North America" in Disguise!) By The Worldwide People's Revolution!® Book 058, who were not exactly the most Ignorant of all Men: beCause, we are still Relying on the Words of Saint Thomas Rebel Jefferson and his Declaration of Interdependence, as well as the Constitution, which used such Capitalized Words, and for Good Reasons; but, not Consistently: beCause, they Obviously Suffered with Chronic Constipation of their Minds; but, not as much as some of their Modern Counterparts, who call themselves "Leaders." Humbug! §§}

45

46

[_] 40-130 — "The Good News According to Saint Andrew!" (A Major Missing Gospel in the Unholy Mutilated Bible!) By Liberty and Justice for ALL! Book 130. It is now Published, and in Color. ISBN — 979-8679-2961-69. {This Inspired Book was once Rejected by Amazon, who Changed their Minds about it, after it was UPDATED, Revised and Modified to Fit the Times. But, that is not to say that the Original Edition cannot be Found somewhere in this World of Wonders: beCause, it can be Found. Just Seek for it, and you can Find it. We Forget just where. Nevertheless, it is one of the Best Books in the Whole World, which has Originality and Enlightenment for whomever has the Faith to Study it. In Fact, it is a Diamond-rated Book, which puts it among the Best of the BEST. Just Try Reeding it, and you will Understand WHY.}

[_] 40-131 — **"This is the Book that Amazon Refused to Publish!" (The Good News According to Saint Andrew!) By The Worldwide People's Revolution!®** Book 131. This Book had to be taken down: beCause, Amazon finally Submitted to Reason and Logic. We figured that they would, if we were Patient and Persistent. They are really not Bad People, in spite of the Fact that some People Think so, who likely got Mistreated by someone who has already been Fired. Perhaps you are one of them, who got Trapped and Abused in the Capitalist System? Whatever the Case, Remember that everyone can Find a Refuge within a Swanky Fortress of one Kind or another, and they will come in all Kinds and Colors. After all, the most Likeable Thing about Swanky Fortresses is their FLEXIBILITY, since each one just Attends to its own Affairs, and leaves all of the others alone. Therefore, if you Find yourself in one that you do not Like, just Move to another one, since all Transportation will be FREE, as well as Communication Systems. Most People within Swanky Fortresses will not really Care much what others are Saying nor Doing. You could actually Liv like a Hermit in a Swanky Fortress, if you Wanted to: beCause, there is no Law against it at some Swanky Fortresses. Just be Sure to Check the Appropriate Box.

[_] 40-132 — "Reading it is Believing it!" (WHY I am the Healthy Happy International HERO of ALL Poor People!) **By The Worldwide People's Revolution!®** Book 132. {NOTE: Since Amazon does not like to Publish our Colored Editions of Books in 8.5 by 11-inches, we are not going to Publish any more Black and White Books for a Time, which are Cheaper, but Inferior. They are simply not worth it. However, we plan on Publishing at least one Cheap Book to give away, which will still Cost $5.50: beCause Amazon has a Minimum Fee, even if the Book is only 32 Pages long: beCause, there are Printing and Handling Costs to Cover. However, if you are Interested in Selling any Books, **The Worldwide People's Revolution** can Obtain BULK Rates, and perhaps for less than 5$ per Book. Contact the E-mail Address on the Back Cover.}

1

[ ] 40-133 — "HOW to DEFEAT Wild Fires, Systematically!" (A Scientific Method for Conquering the Enemy!) **By The Worldwide People's Revolution!®** Book 133. This Inspired Book contains Top Secret Information, which neither the Fire Department, nor the Fake Federal Government wants you to Learn, not to Mention the Worthless Insurance Companies, Selfish Bankers, nor Greedy Lawyers, who gain a lot of Money from the Ignorance of People, who are otherwise known as "Modern Deceived SLAVES!" (10 Simple Steps for Liberating ALL Modern Slaves, Worldwide, Including Yourself!) **By Liberty and Justice for ALL!** Book 113. This Book is a bit "Pricy," as they say; but, a Church can easily Afford it by Pooling their Resources; and so could all Fire Departments, if they Wanted to "Waste a little Money." We can See where they have already Wasted TRILLIONS of Dollars! ‡

16
17

[ ] 40-134 — "What Unites People?" (HOW People can be Reunited Properly!) **By The Worldwide People's Revolution!®** Book 134. {It has been sed that no Nation on the Entire Earth is so Divided as the so-called "United States of North America," which has mostly been Divided by the Fake Trumpeter and his Gang of Outlaws; but, there is something that Unites People, which is Revealed within this Inspired Book; and, yes, it does Require some LOVE; but, mostly just Honesty, which Requires some Humility, which even a Mule has, who is not Afraid to Kiss the Man with a Beard. In Fact, that Mule probably Likes Beards and Robes. You would Like them also, if you just Wore them for a Time or 2: beCause, Robes have more than 77 Advantages for Men. For Example, you cannot Forget to Zip Up your Pants, nor can your Pants Fall Off.}

32

33

[ ] 40-135 — "Super Debate!" (Trump and Biden Debate our Selected King with Jesus Christ Moderating!) **By The Worldwide People's Revolution!®** Book 135. {It is actually one of the Best Books in the Whole World: beCause our Selected King Wins the Debate, just beCause Jesus Christ is Moderating it, instead of Chris Wallace. Therefore, it has a Fantastic Ending, and those 2 Roosters are Sent Packing with their Empty Bags. So, before there are any more Worthless Debates, everyone should Study this Exceptionally Good Book, whereby they might Learn Provable Truths.}

[_] 40-136 — "HOW to Conquer the World by Constructing GLORIOUS HOTELS!" (A Peaceful Takeover of the Evil Empires!) **By The Worldwide People's Revolution!® Book 136.** {It is a Simple and Highly-Workable Idea, once you See the Vision of it. Maybe North Korea will take up the Idea, and Run with it? Even Poor Little Cuba could Do it, if they had the Faith to get it going! Indeed, any Rich Church or Organization could do it, if they would. ‡}

[_] 40-137 — "The Affordable Constitutional Health Care Act!" (A New Amendment to the Constitution for the United States of North America!) **By The Worldwide People's Revolution!® Book 137.** {This Inspired Book contains a very Special Chapter 08, wherein God Explains Certain Mysteries, which Unravel Ancient Questions, which makes this one of the Best Books on the Whole Earth. Therefore, if you Want to Satisfy the Belly of your Mind, this is just for YOU. Remember that it is Guaranteed to Satisfy you. Amazon will Refund your Money on any Books, if you are not Satisfied.}

[_] 40-138 — "I did NOT Vote!" (There are 7 Billion Reasons!) **By The Worldwide People's Revolution!® Book 138.** {Some People are Shocked to Learn that about half of Americans never Vote, and especially if they are very Religious People, who take God Seriously: beCause, we are Partakers of the Sins of the People whom we Vote for. Therefore, if you Voted for the Fake Trumpeter, for Example, you are a Partaker of his Sins, and will Answer to God for it during the Day of his Judgments. Therefore, you can now Understand the Seriousness of this Subject, which should Inspire you to Reed the Book, and "VOTE for The GOAT!" (The New Political Party that has Guaranteed Solutions for our Massive Problems!) By The Worldwide People's Revolution!® Book 109.}

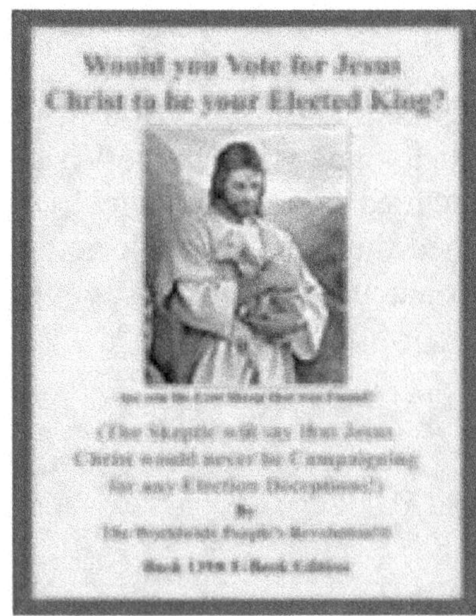

15

[_] 40-139 — "Would you Vote for Jesus Christ to be your Elected King?" (The Skeptic will say that Jesus Christ would never be Campaigning for any Election Deceptions!) **By The Worldwide People's Revolution!®** Book 139. {You might Think that it is just a Joke; but, it is not. Would Jesus Want to Govern a World that did not Love him? Do you Love him? Would you Vote for him? Have you Studied all of his Commandments, and Agree to Love and Obey them? If so, why are you still Driving that Stinking, Noisy, Polluting and DANGEROUS Car? Why are you Contributing to the Destruction of our World, which is Actually his World? Knowing that, most People would probably NOT Vote for Jesus. Would you be Willing to Liv in a Swanky Fortress which has no Cars, which uses Elevators, Escalators and Electric Trains?}

30

[_] 40-140 — "The World from THEIR Point of View!" (Who will Speak for the Masses of People, who have no Voice in Government?) **By The Worldwide People's Revolution!®** Book 140. {You may Call the *Washington Journal* on the C-SPAN Network, and Share your Honest Opinion about something, if you Address their given Subject or Question; but, what about the Questions that the Hosts of the *Washington Journal* never Ask? What about the Hordes of People, who Liv in Remote Jungles and Wilderness Areas of the World? Who Speaks for them? Who even knows what their Problems are? Do they have Tools to Work with? Do they have Water to Work with? Do their Teeths need Repairing? Who is Caring for them? Should they be left to Care for themselves? Are their Problems our Problems? How does God Feel about all of these Things? ‡}

42

[_] 40-141 — "The Peabrain Peacock Studies Demon-ocracy!" (A Guaranteed Solution for the Plastic Trash Problem!) **By The Worldwide People's Revolution!®** Book 141. Every Educated Person in the Whole World knows for a Fact that Capitalists have a Major Trash Problem, which the Founding Fathers did not Visualize, or else they might have Changed their Minds about Allowing the Ignorant Children to have so many Freedoms, whereby they Exploit the Natural Resources, and leave their own Great Grandchildren with nothing but Trash Dumps and Burned Out Forests to Inherit. Just why they are Determined to make Fools of themselves is a bit of a Mystery. However, the Apostle Paul called it *"... the Love of Money, which is the Root Cause for almost all Evils."* — *First Timothy 6 something.*

43
44
45
46

[_] 40-142 — "King David Lives Again!" (WHY Americans, and the Wise People of the Whole World, Want a Righteous KING to Govern them!) **By The Worldwide People's Revolution!®** Book 142.

1 {NOTE: That Long List of Available Books will be Updated, Periodically, if we do not get Killed
2 by some Thugs, who Work for those Lying Conniving Edomites! You may use this Page for
3 making your Personal Notes. After all, it is your Personal Book, and you are Free to Do whatever
4 you Want with it; but, there is a Good Chance that one of your Poor Naaberz might Appreciate it.}
5
6
7

www.ingramcontent.com/pod-product-compliance
Lightning Source LLC
Chambersburg PA
CBHW081341160726
48000CB00010B/3191